CREATING SELF-REGULATED LEARNERS

CREATING SELF-REGULATED LEARNERS

Strategies to Strengthen Students' Self-Awareness and Learning Skills

Linda B. Nilson

Foreword by Barry J. Zimmerman

STERLING, VIRGINIA

Published by Stylus Publishing, LLC
22883 Quicksilver Drive
Sterling, Virginia 20166-2102

Library of Congress Cataloging-in-Publication Data
Nilson, Linda Burzotta
Creating self-regulated learners : strategies to
strengthen students' self-awareness and learning skills /
Linda B. Nilson.
p.   cm. —
Includes bibliographical references and index.
ISBN 978-1-57922-866-8 (cloth : alk. paper)
ISBN 978-1-57922-867-5 (pbk. : alk. paper)
ISBN 978-1-57922-868-2 (library networkable e-edition)
ISBN 978-1-57922-869-9 (consumer e-edition)
1. Learning.   2. Self-control.   3. Study skills.   I. Title.
LB1060.N55 2013
370.15'23—dc23
                                                    2013009090

13-digit ISBN: 978-1-57922-866-8 (cloth)
13-digit ISBN: 978-1-57922-867-5 (paperback)
13-digit ISBN: 978-1-57922-868-2 (library networkable e-edition)
13-digit ISBN: 978-1-57922-869-9 (consumer e-edition)

Printed in the United States of America

All first editions printed on acid-free paper
that meets the American National Standards Institute
Z39-48 Standard.

Bulk Purchases

Quantity discounts are available for use in workshops and for
staff development.
Call 1-800-232-0223

First Edition, 2013

10   9

To Greg,

who frees my mind, heart, and time to write.

CONTENTS

QUICK REFERENCE TO SELF-REGULATED LEARNING ASSIGNMENTS AND ACTIVITIES DESCRIBED IN THIS BOOK

For the Beginning of a Course

Assignment or Activity	Type of Grading Required	Estimated Class Time Required or Homework (HW)	Content Related?	Comments	Book Pages
Class discussion on reading about learning/thinking	None	15–20 min.	No		15–17
Writing answers to questions on reading about learning/thinking	Specifications (explained in chapter 10)	HW, and can launch 20+ min. class discussion	No		17
Writing course goals	Specifications	3 min., and can launch 10 min. class discussion	No	Prompts: Why are you in this course? What are your goals?	17
"How I Earned an A in This Course" essay	Specifications	HW, and can launch 10–15 min. discussion	No	Option to repeat at end of course	17
Class brainstorming on ways to earn an A in the course	None	10 min.; 15 min. with groups and class sharing	No		18

Assignment or Activity	Type of Grading Required	Estimated Class Time Required or Homework (HW)	Content Related?	Comments	Book Pages
Self-assessment of self-regulated learning skills	Specifications	5–10 min., and can launch 10 min. class discussion	No	Metacognitive Activities Inventory, Metacognitive Awareness Inventory, or questions on how one learns Best to repeat at end of course	18–20
Self-assessment of course knowledge and skills	Specifications	5–20 min.	Yes	Reflective or content-focused writing Option to repeat at end of course, when it can be the final exam	20–22
Knowledge survey	Specifications	5–20 min.	Yes	Best to repeat at end of course	22–24

For **During** a Course

Assignment or Activity	Type of Grading Required	Estimated Class Time Required or Homework (HW)	Content Related?	Comments	Book Pages
Reflective writing on assigned readings, videos, or podcasts	Specifications	HW	Yes	Questions about how one learns, study cycle questions, free-written summaries, personal reactions, minute papers Also assures HW compliance	26–28
Writing answers to genre content or study questions on readings, videos, or podcasts	Specifications	HW	Yes	Also assures HW compliance	28–30
Student-developed exam questions on readings, videos, or podcasts	Specifications	30 min. to learn how to do and practice in groups, then 5–10 min./visual or HW	Yes	Typically multiple-choice or multiple true-false items	29–30
Self-testing in recall-and-review on readings, videos, or podcasts	None	HW	Yes	For example, SQ3R or PQR3	30—31

Assignment or Activity	Type of Grading Required	Estimated Class Time Required or Homework (HW)	Content Related?	Comments	Book Pages
Retrieval-practice quizzes and mind dumps on readings, videos, or podcasts	Specifications	5–15 min., and can launch 5–10 min. class discussion or group work	Yes	Also assures HW compliance	31—32
Visual representations of readings, videos, or podcasts	Specifications	30 min. to learn how to do and practice in groups, then 5–10 min./visual or HW	Yes	Maps, diagrams, flowcharts, matrices	32–35
Prelecture: Active knowledge sharing	None	10–15 min.	Yes		37–38
Clicker questions during lecture	None	3 min./question including peer instruction	Yes	Conceptual questions are best	38
Student questions identified by level (Bloom's taxonomy)	None	1–3 min.	Yes		39
Pair and group activities during lecture	None	2–15 min. depending on activity	Yes		39–40
Quick-thinks lecture-break activities	None	1–5 min.	Yes		40—41

(Continued)

Assignment or Activity	Type of Grading Required	Estimated Class Time Required or Homework (HW)	Content Related?	Comments	Book Pages
Pair activities to close lecture	None	2–4 min.	Yes	Closure note-taking pairs, pair review	41
Student-developed exam questions to close lecture	Specifications	5–10 min.	Yes		42
Minute paper to close lecture	Specifications	1–3 min.	Yes		42–43
RSQC2 to close lecture	Specifications	5–6 min.	Yes		43
Active listening checks to close lecture	Specifications	3–4 min.	Yes		43–44
Visual representations of lectures	Specifications	30 min. to learn how to do and practice in groups, then 5–10 min./visual or HW	Yes	Maps, diagrams, flowcharts, matrices	44–45
Meta-assignments on mathematically based problems	Specifications	HW	Yes	Confidence assessment, error analysis	47–48

Assignment or Activity	Type of Grading Required	Estimated Class Time Required or Homework (HW)	Content Related?	Comments	Book Pages
Think Aloud on HW problems in pairs	None	5–10 min.	Yes		48
Meta-assignments on authentic fuzzy problems	Specifications or rubric	HW	Yes	Description of thinking process	48–51
Reflective meta-assignments on experiential learning; service-learning, fieldwork, internships, simulations, and role-plays	Specifications or rubric	HW	Yes	Prompts depend on assignment	51–54
Meta-assignments on papers and projects	Specifications	HW	Yes	Description of research process, problems overcome, skills acquired, self-assessment of work, self-development, revision plans, paraphrase of instructor feedback, letter to next class about assignment	54–56

(Continued)

Assignment or Activity	Type of Grading Required	Estimated Class Time Required or Homework (HW)	Content Related?	Comments	Book Pages
Meta-assignments on portfolios	Specifications or rubric	HW	Yes	Prompts depend on kind of portfolio	56–58
Student-developed exam questions to prepare for exams	Specifications	1–10 min./question or HW	Yes		61
Student-created review sheets/test blueprints for exams	Specifications	30–40 min. or HW	Yes		62
Preexam knowledge survey on exam material	Specifications	5–10 min.	Yes		63
Self-confidence ratings during exams	Specifications	5–10 sec./problem	Yes		63–64
Postquiz reflection and self-assessment in pairs or groups	None	3–8 min.	Yes		64
Postquiz or postexam written corrections and reflections	Specifications	10–45 min.	Yes		64–67

Assignment or Activity	Type of Grading Required	Estimated Class Time Required or Homework (HW)	Content Related?	Comments	Book Pages
Immediate postexam written self-assessment	Specifications	3–8 min.	Yes		68–69
Post-graded-exam self-assessment	Specifications	10–15 min.	Yes		69
Study game plan for next exam	Specifications	5 min./plan	No		69
Test autopsy	Specifications	5–10 min.	Yes		69–71
Reasoning practice (after instructor models) in pairs or groups	None	20–30 min. including instructor modeling	Yes		73–74
Frequent knowledge surveys	Specifications	3–5 min./survey	Yes		74
Frequent online metacognition discussions	Specifications	Online/HW	No		74–75

(Continued)

Assignment or Activity	Type of Grading Required	Estimated Class Time Required or Homework (HW)	Content Related?	Comments	Book Pages
Weekly journaling on learning	Specifications	HW	No		75
Occasional reflective writing assignments	Specifications	HW	Yes		75–77
Writing assignments to encourage deferring gratification	Specifications	HW	No		81–82
Writing assignments to overcome procrastination	Specifications	HW	No		83–85

For the End of a Course

Assignment or Activity	Type of Grading Required	Estimated Class Time Required or Homework (HW)	Content Related?	Comments	Book Pages
"How I Earned an A in This Course—or Not" essay	Specifications	HW	No	Option to pair with "How I Earned an A in This Course" essay at beginning of course	86–87
Self-assessment of self-regulated learning skills	Specifications	5–10 min., and can launch 10 min. class discussion	No	Metacognitive Activities Inventory, Metacognitive Awareness Inventory, or questions on how one learns

Best to give at beginning of course as well | 87 |

(Continued)

Assignment or Activity	Type of Grading Required	Estimated Class Time Required or Homework (HW)	Content Related?	Comments	Book Pages
Self-assessment of course knowledge and skills	Rubric	15 min. for group work and individual writing as HW Up to 2 hours if final exam	Yes	Reflective writing on subject matter or content-focused writing, such as letter to pre-class self or "value-added" essay final Best or essential to give at beginning of course as well	87–88
Knowledge survey	Specifications	5–20 min.	Yes	Best to give at beginning of course as well	88
Skills grid	Specifications	10–15 min. or HW	Yes		89
"Future Uses" paper	Rubric	HW	Yes		88–89
Letter to the next cohort	Specifications	HW	No		89–90

FOREWORD

The origins of interest in academic self-regulation can be traced in part to an initial meeting of the Studying and Self-Regulated Learning Special Interest Group (SIG) during an annual convention of the American Educational Research Association (AERA). The issue of studying had been given little attention at the time, but Bill Rohwer (1984) had just written an article in the *Educational Psychologist* lamenting this oversight. The inclusion of "self-regulated learning" in the title of the SIG was due to the growing awareness of a key issue: For studying methods to be sustained and transferred, they should be investigated in conjunction with self-regulatory processes. These processes included sources of motivation (e.g., self-efficacy beliefs, delay of gratification, attributions, and values/interests) as well as sources of metacognition (e.g., goal setting, strategy use, self-monitoring, and self-evaluation).

Linda Nilson, who has long been at the forefront of instructional applications of self-regulated learning, advances our understanding of the processes and offers practical guidance on how to apply them. I was particularly taken with Linda's account of her private Catholic girls' school education where her teachers closely monitored her acquisition of the course material. Her mastery of that material was tested individually and publicly in class, which led her to develop self-regulatory techniques to survive in this challenging academic environment. As a youth, I too developed self-regulatory study techniques to deal with taxing instructional contexts. When I entered the first year of junior high school (the seventh grade), I vividly remember facing greatly increased assignments, demanding examinations, and public honor roll grading that was announced in the local newspaper. To meet these new demanding academic standards, I began taking notes regarding class lectures and reading assignments, synthesizing and reorganizing these notes in preparation for examinations, and going over exam results to see if missed questions had been covered in my note-taking system. Thus, for both Linda and me, self-regulation arose from necessity, not from mere awareness of or vague intentions to use these processes. I was particularly attracted to Linda's book due to her provision of a functional path to self-regulatory knowledge and methods of instruction.

There are many attractive features of this book for students as well as their teachers. For example, Linda distinguishes self-regulation from related constructs such as metacognition, deliberate practice, and emotional control based on the latest research and theory. She defines *self-regulation* in temporal terms—namely, processes and beliefs that precede, accompany, and follow efforts to learn, which in turn affect subsequent cycles of learning. This temporal approach to self-regulated learning has important benefits for both students and teachers, such as producing increases in students' achievement, depth and scope of reasoning, conscious focus on learning, and enhanced self-reflection. Finally, she describes instructional methods designed to facilitate students' development of a self-regulatory approach to learning. These included "meta-assignments" that involved recording one's thinking and actions and "wrappers," which are activities and assignments that direct students' attention to self-regulation before, during, or after learning regular course components. Linda provides instructional suggestions for converting common reactive learning activities such as reading, watching, and listening into proactive activities through the temporal use of self-regulated learning processes.

In addition to describing students' studying from a temporal perspective on self-regulation, Linda also discusses their quiz and exam performance temporally. For example, during test preparation, she provides examples of how students can prepare better by estimating their confidence in their knowledge of specific components of the course, such as words on a spelling list. During the course of testing, students can reassess their confidence in their answers by self-monitoring their efforts to learn. After the tests are graded, students can compare their initial confidence judgments with their actual results. Misjudgments of confidence can be identified and erroneous solution strategies can be corrected. Linda provides many examples of self-regulatory record keeping forms that can be used to guide students on how to interpret their exam results.

Finally, I greatly enjoyed Linda's discussion of various creative methods for grading students' work from a self-regulative perspective. I was especially impressed with her allowance of additional opportunities for students to make up points by correcting errors on quizzes and with her advocacy of a mastery scoring system that allows students extra chances to learn specific course objectives to a high level of proficiency (e.g., 90%). These self-regulatory methods of grading are designed to change students' perceptions of their errors from signs of imperfection to opportunities to enhance learning. Clearly the literature on self-regulated learning has made important strides in recent years, and Linda Nilson is an especially able guide—providing her readers many compelling examples of how it can be fostered instructionally.

Barry J. Zimmerman
Professor Emeritus of Educational Psychology
City University of New York

Reference

Rohwer, W. D. (1984). An invitation to an educational psychology of studying. *Educational Psychologist, 19*(1), 1–14.

PREFACE

W ho would be interested in creating self-regulated learners? This question could be rephrased as, "Who is interested in learning?" because deep, lasting learning of any subject matter requires self-regulation. So does critical thinking, because it entails the reflective, questioning examination of one's beliefs, values, conclusions, and thinking processes. So does the acquisition of skills, whether mental or physical, because productive practice demands objective self-observation and self-evaluation as well as motivation and perseverance. As a result, this book should obviously prove highly informative to college and university faculty as well as secondary-school teachers. Those involved in developing faculty may want to use it to develop their own training workshops and materials and to advise their clients on how to help students achieve course and program learning outcomes more successfully. While the text is directed to these readers, students would be wise to peruse it to find out how their mind learns and how to make it learn more effectively. In fact, I wrote every word in this book with the ultimate intention of helping an externally oriented generation of students turn inward and realize that learning is an inside job.

This book started with a chance exchange some years ago. Dr. Lydia Schleifer, associate professor of accounting in Clemson University's School of Accountancy and Finance, suggested that I do a workshop on self-regulated learning. As director of the Office of Teaching Effectiveness and Innovation, developing and conducting teaching workshops for faculty was and still is my job. I had heard of *self-regulated learning* but really didn't know much about it. Figuring I might be able to find an outside speaker to meet Lydia's needs, I googled the term and came up with some researchers' names—Dr. Barry Zimmerman's prominent among them. But I couldn't get a hold of anyone, and I recall that Dr. Zimmerman was in Europe at the time. So I shelved self-regulated learning for the time being.

Then I started hearing and reading about metacognition—in particular, how chemistry professor and learning center director Dr. Saundra McGuire was applying it to work turnaround miracles with failing students at Louisiana State University. Had she found the magic bullet? A few months later I heard that some geologists were infusing their courses with metacognitive activities and assignments. Metacognition led me to self-regulated learning, which turned out to be the broader of the two topics. The latter encompassed not only the former but behaviors as well: self-discipline, deferring gratification, and starting tasks early instead of procrastinating. These behaviors and meta-cognition seemed to be the ultimate study skills for every learner and the ingredients of life success, and today's students had them in short supply.

When I looked back on my school years I realized I was practicing self-regulated learning starting in the sixth grade or earlier. The private Catholic girls' school I attended from the third through eighth grades assigned enormous amounts of homework and had recitation on a good deal of it every day. The nun would cold-call on one of us—and classes were small—to stand up and recite poetry we were supposed to have memorized or answer questions about the textbook chapter we had been assigned to read. I accustomed myself to a daily life of classroom terror and actually excelled in that environment. Not that I would wish it on any child, but I can't imagine who I would be or what I'd be doing if I hadn't been subjected to it. My drive to survive made me learn self-regulation early. How else could I be prepared for any possible question the nun could throw at me without testing myself after every section of text? How else could I master the "new math" without monitoring my understanding of set theory and numerical base theory? How else could I face having to regurgitate multiplication tables, French verb conjugations, and historical names and dates in front of all my classmates without first evaluating how quickly and accurately I could recall them?

The self-discipline component went along with the work. To finish my nightly homework, I had to start it right after dinner and work up until 11:00 p.m. or midnight. Then I often stayed up another hour just to do what the child in me wanted to do, like write short plays. With every weekend also came a substantial writing assignment—a composition or formal letter—about which I might procrastinate until Sunday afternoon and pay for it with a worrisome Saturday. But unless I was willing to look like a fool in class, I couldn't afford to procrastinate any work for very long. High school with all its honors, advanced honors, and college-level courses was just more of the same but without the cold-calling. So I wound up deferring my gratification until college, which, after what I had been through, was pretty easy and straightforward.

Most of today's young students grow up in a considerably different parental and school environment. Because many schools focus on building self-esteem, few students face daily public accountability for doing their homework, if they are even assigned any. In many cases, they receive passing grades without passing scores, honors without excelling in their coursework, and the aura of achievement without earning it. Sadly, these students do not have the opportunity in secondary school to learn how to learn. Now in college, they do not realize that reading involves interacting with the text and evaluating one's comprehension of it, that studying for a test means testing oneself, and that writing a paper requires advance planning and goal setting.

Society has yet to pay the full price for this misdirected socialization. But colleges and universities have been struggling with more than a generation of poorly prepared students who have succeeded in pressuring institutions and its instructors to lower standards, dilute rigor, trim down homework, and cater to the tastes of the millennial generation. Except for the most educationally privileged and motivated, these students know little about self-regulation and therefore little about learning. Study skills really aren't the point. Learning is about one's relationship with oneself and one's ability to exert the effort, self-control, and critical self-assessment necessary to achieve the best possible results—and about overcoming risk aversion, failure, distractions, and sheer laziness in pursuit of *real* achievement. This is self-regulated learning.

ACKNOWLEDGMENTS

While writing this book I was a member of a Clemson University writing group for faculty and graduate students that held me accountable for meeting my productivity goals every two weeks—and forgave me when I didn't. Actually, I have organized and led these groups every semester and summer for the past several years. Feeling that I should be a good role model reinforced my motivation. So I would like to thank the members of the spring, summer, and fall 2012 writing groups for being there, because that alone applied just the right amount of pressure.

Colleagues can be perfect strangers one moment and the most open and helpful friends the next. To obtain more information about their research and classroom experiments than their publications and recorded presentations furnished, I contacted these people out of the blue: Dr. John Hudesman, Center for Advanced Study in Education (CASE) in the Graduate Center at the City University of New York (CUNY); Sara Crosby, former writing instructor at New York City College of Technology and now assistant director of academic affairs at Kingsborough Community College (CUNY); Dr. Dexter Perkins, professor of geology at the University of North Dakota; and Dr. Karl Wirth, professor of geology at Macalester College. These wonderful folks took time out from their busy days to talk with and e-mail me, supplying important additional information about their studies, their teaching innovations, and their results that was available nowhere else. Of course, I thank Clemson University accounting professor Lydia Schleifer for pointing me toward the topic of self-regulated learning to begin with. Dr. John ("Mike") Coggeshall, professor of anthropology at Clemson University, has been a friend of mine for some time. A number of years ago, he started measuring his students' learning pre- and postcourse and submitting this information for his faculty reviews, and I invited him to present his innovative approach during my workshops on measuring student learning. What he does has value as a self-regulated learning assignment as well, since his students have the opportunity to compare their uninformed beliefs and thinking at the beginning of the course with their knowledgeable, evidence-based reasoning at the end. I am pleased to share his strategy here.

This book offered my first opportunity to work with John von Knorring, my editor and president of Stylus Publishing, and it was a very productive one. He attended my session on self-regulated learning at the October 2011 conference of the Professional and Organizational Development (POD) Network in Higher Education in Atlanta. Right afterward he approached me saying that he wanted me to write a book on the topic and that it could pave the way for another book on grading that he knew I wanted to write. I asked him to give me a month or two to try the topic on for size, which meant to start outlining the manuscript. Could it consume me with enough passion to complete a book? It seemed it could. So after finishing the outline, I started sculpting each chapter, phrase by phrase, sentence by sentence. Within less than a year, it was done—many months early. (The nuns would have been proud!) When I sent him the first draft of this book, I didn't expect to hear from him for at least weeks, definitely not until after the holidays. But he was back to me in two days with excellent revision ideas. Literally *all* of his suggestions made sense to me and would clearly improve the clarity, usability, and overall richness of the manuscript. I dove right into the revisions and looked forward to the book appearing a year earlier than I originally expected. My relationship with John has been incredibly fruitful, amiable, and gratifying.

My deepest thanks go to my husband, Greg, who worked behind the scenes to free my time and mind to write this book. He deftly handles those time-consuming details of everyday life—the endless errands, the grocery shopping, most of the cooking, the house repairs and improvements, and the heavy lawn and garden work—so that I can work. He encouraged me all through the project, even though it took time away from us, and celebrated every completed chapter with me. When people ask me how I seem to get so much done, I simply point to him. So it is only right that I dedicate this book to him.

WHAT IS SELF-REGULATED LEARNING AND HOW DOES IT ENHANCE LEARNING?

A major goal of higher education is to create lifelong learners—intentional, independent, self-directed learners who can acquire, retain, and retrieve new knowledge on their own (American Association of Colleges and Universities, 2002, 2007; Wirth, 2008a). Only lifelong learners will be able to keep up with the explosive growth of knowledge and skills in their career and to retool into a new career after their previous one runs its course. This need to retool is already a reality in this society—witness the unprecedented expansion in adult education and the high unemployment rate among workers who haven't met this challenge—and it will become the norm for this generation of traditional-age students as well as subsequent ones. Turning our students into lifelong learners no longer translates into the academic ideal of producing widely read cultural elites, but rather equipping our graduates with basic economic survival skills. We *owe* our students lessons and practice in how to learn at a fairly high level; letting them slip through college without solid learning skills and, subsequently, with only fleetingly superficial knowledge is professionally irresponsible, if not unethical.

Yet few of our students show the signs of being intentional, independent, self-directed learners.

Our Students as Learners

A recent study asked 132 veterinary students to identify the factors that they considered important in their learning (Ruohoniemi & Lindblom-Ylänne, 2009). They most commonly cited the planning and practices of the instruction they were receiving, including the workload in their courses and the curriculum as a whole. The respondents—and remember that these are professional students—rarely named their own effort, learning skills, or study methods. As they perceived it, learning was something that was happening to them, and the faculty's job was to make it happen. These learners were not at all intentional, independent, or self-directed.

Not surprisingly, research on younger undergraduate students reveals the same mind-set. Specifically, these students take little or no responsibility for their own learning, blaming their shortcomings in achievement on their "ineffective" instruction and the "too advanced" or irrelevant course material (e.g., Elliott, 2010; Singleton-Jackson, Jackson, & Reinhardt, 2010; Twenge, 2007). Furthermore, they admit to having little or no interest in learning, certainly not for learning's sake (Pryor, Hurtado, DeAngelo, Palucki Blake, & Tran, 2011), which no doubt broadens their definition of *irrelevant*. Reinforcing their avoidance of responsibility for their learning is their widespread belief that learning should not require effort. Effort didn't seem necessary in elementary and high school, where many of them received credit just for showing up, so why should learning require so much time and hard work now? They are speaking from twelve years of experience in school, more than half their lives, making their expectations quite reasonable. These students were also led to believe that they were born smart, furnishing another justification for their not having to work hard. First, their parents created this self-concept; their schools then added to the notion by awarding trophies indiscriminately to everyone (Elliott, 2010). Therefore, learning, along with strong reading comprehension and communication skills, should come quickly and easily. If they don't, students logically reason, the fault lies with the instructor or with their own lack of flair for the particular subject matter. If they attribute their problem to the latter, most of them still figure that there's no use in trying hard, let alone persevering, because they were born that way. In other words, they have been socialized into accepting a fixed-intelligence mind-set (Dweck, 2007), a belief that actually had currency until the neurocognitive research showed otherwise during the past decade.

Given their beliefs about the sources of their achievement, our students understandably lack certain kinds of knowledge about learning, cognitive tasks, and the way the mind processes and stores new input. In the language of the self-regulated learning literature, they have little of the following kinds of knowledge (Hofer, Yu, & Pintrich, 1998; Pintrich, 2002; Pintrich, McKeachie, & Lin, 1987):

- *Strategic knowledge*, which encompasses knowledge of the following: different learning strategies and heuristics for different types of tasks; the steps and algorithms needed for solving problems and executing technical tasks; the need to plan, monitor, and evaluate their learning and thinking; and effective strategies for rehearsal (memorizing), elaboration (using learning devices such as summarizing, paraphrasing, and linking new knowledge to prior knowledge), and organization of the material (such as concept mapping).

- *Knowledge about cognitive tasks*, which includes comprehending the directions (such as knowing what the verbs mean), assessing the difficulty of the task, and deciding wisely which learning and thinking strategies to use when.

- *Self-knowledge*, which entails knowing one's strengths and weaknesses as a learner, accurately judging one's command of the material, and knowing what strategies work best for oneself to accomplish given tasks.

We may have acquired these skills along the way, but we are professional learners. Without these abilities, we might not have advanced so far in the education system. But few of our students have been taught these in the past or have picked them up on their own, as some of us did. Is it any wonder that students rarely have questions on the readings and lectures? They do not know what they have and have not understood, and so they optimistically assume that they have understood and will therefore remember the material. Learning does not work this way, but they know neither how learning works nor what they have to do to ensure it.

The literature on self-regulated learning tells us that deep, lasting, independent learning requires a range of activities—cognitive, affective, and even physical—that go far beyond reading and listening. It entails, first, setting learning goals for a class period, assignment, or study session. Then the learner must plan how to go about the task effectively—perhaps actively listening, taking notes, outlining, visually representing the material, occasionally self-quizzing, reviewing, or writing a summary. While executing the plan, she must direct and control her focus and behavior to stay on task, but allowing herself appropriate short breaks for revitalizing her brain. At the same time, she must observe and monitor her mind and actions to ensure that they aren't succumbing to distraction, fatigue, discouragement, or detrimental self-talk ("I'm just no good at _____"). She has to maintain and reinforce her motivation to learn this material, perhaps by considering its relevance to her experiences or her future. If her mind wanders from the task, she has to bring herself back to it. She also has to be aware of how well she is understanding and absorbing the material by occasionally pausing to evaluate her command of it. Can she paraphrase the most important points? Can she perceive and organize the interrelationships among them? Are her learning strategies and schedule working for her? If not, how can she regulate them to achieve better results—not only this time, but the next time she tackles a similar task?

In short, self-regulated learning is a total-engagement activity involving multiple parts of the brain. This activity encompasses full attention and concentration, self-awareness and introspection, honest self-assessment, openness to change, genuine self-discipline, and acceptance of responsibility for one's learning (Zimmerman, 2001, 2002; Zimmerman & Schunk, 2001). These components sound more like dimensions of character than cognitive ability. Indeed, the literature contends that self-regulation has little to do with measured intelligence and just about anyone can develop it (R. J. Davidson, 2003; Schraw, 1998; Schraw & Dennison, 1994; Schunk & Zimmerman, 1998; Tinnesz, Ahuna, & Kiener, 2006). In fact, social cognitive psychologists studying how children developed self-control conducted the initial research on self-regulation, going back to the early 1960s. They found that response inhibition, the ability to delay gratification, and the acquisition of self-regulating norms furnished the basis for self-control. Given these terms, the literature seems to suggest that character, or at least some aspects of it, plays a major role in defining *self-regulated learning*.

Self-control, self-discipline, perseverance, and determination in pursuing long-term goals outweigh IQ as predictors of postsecondary academic success and, among children, performance on a spelling bee (Duckworth, Peterson, Matthews, & Kelly, 2007; Duckworth & Seligman, 2005; Tough, 2012). Anyone who has completed a PhD would probably agree these traits are more important than just being bright. Also critical to academic achievement is the ability to delay gratification, which a considerable literature finds closely associated with self-efficacy beliefs and reassurances, intrinsic motivation, perceived task value, a "mastery" or "learning" (versus performance) goal orientation, help seeking, use of proven cognitive learning strategies (rehearsal, elaboration, organization, and metacognition), and control of study-related behavior and environment (see next section) (Bembenutty, 2011). All this research strengthens the case that self-regulated learning is interwoven with a constellation of behavioral practices, values, beliefs, and personal traits, some of which fall under the umbrella of *character*.

Why don't our students come to college with these aspects of character? We can point to various suspects in their past, but it really doesn't matter who or what may be at fault. We have these young people now, and if we do not help them make up for the shortfalls of their socialization, they will not learn what they will need to become contributing citizens, wise consumers of goods and information, productive workers, and survivors of what promises to be an economically and technologically volatile future. To date we have been doing too little to help students acquire self-regulation skills and assume responsibility for their learning (Zimmerman, 2002).

Self-Regulation Versus Metacognition

You may very well be familiar with the concept of metacognition and may be wondering whether it and self-regulation are the same thing. My unequivocal answer is "yes and no." While some may disagree, self-regulation is the more general concept, and metacognition is a major facet of it (Husman, 2008). Specifically, metacognition is one's conscious control over one's *cognitive* processes—such as focusing on given input, dialoguing with it, observing one's preconceptions and consequent resistance to novel or conflicting inputs, and reviewing and reflecting on an experience (Husman, 2008). Zimmerman (2002) calls *metacognition* "the awareness and knowledge about one's own thinking" (p. 65), and Schraw (1998) defines it as thinking about how one performs a skill. Recall from the previous section the types of knowledge that most students lack: strategic knowledge, knowledge about cognitive tasks, and self-knowledge, at least as far as learning is concerned (Pintrich, 2002)—types of metacognitive knowledge. From whatever perspective, metacognition involves self-feedback on one's learning, an essential component of meaningful learning and transfer (Bransford, Brown, & Cocking, 2000; Schraw, 1998).

In contrast, self-regulation encompasses the monitoring and managing of one's cognitive processes as well as the awareness of and control over one's emotions, motivations, behavior, and environment as related to learning. *Behavior* includes self-discipline; effort; time management; and when deemed necessary, help seeking from the instructor or some other more knowledgeable party (Karabenick & Dembo, 2011). *Environment* encompasses the use of technology, task management (single tasking versus multitasking), and sensory inputs, such as place, temperature, background sounds (e.g., music), and physical position. A learner has to find out what kind of environment works best for her learning. The process starts with self-observation and task-oriented self-talk, as in talking one's way through a new task. The learner must experiment with and observe the effects of various emotions, motivations, behaviors, environments, and cognitive processes and decide which ones maximize or impede learning. Those with positive effects tend to reduce the cognitive load while she is engaged in learning (Husman, 2008). Finally, the learner must exercise self-control in creating the optimal cognitive, affective, and physical settings and the best schedule for her learning.

Most of our younger students have not mastered these processes. In addition to their poor metacognitive skills, they have issues with regulating their motivation and emotions, controlling their study-related behavior, and making wise decisions about their learning environment. On the affective level, many have trouble deferring gratification, shutting out competing stimuli, motivating themselves to tackle hard tasks, and maintaining the self-confidence and longer-term outlook needed to persevere. They typically externalize their locus of control, take a passive view of learning, feel entitled to academic rewards for modest effort, and have an inflated, unearned sense of self-esteem. Behaviorally their self-discipline and time management skills are weak, and they subvert their learning environment with social and technological distractions and multiple-task rotation (Bauerlein, 2008; Dweck, 2007; Lancaster & Stillman, 2003; Nathan, 2005; Pintrich, 2002; Pryor et al., 2011; Singleton-Jackson, Jackson, & Reinhardt, 2010; Twenge, 2007). Of course, these apparent behavioral weaknesses may reflect the higher priority that students are giving to their jobs, social life, family, athletic development, or something else. Still, we have a lot of work to do to transform these young people into self-directed lifelong learners.

Self-Regulation Versus Deliberate Practice

A concept in psychological research that is similar to self-regulated learning is *deliberate practice*. Ericsson, Krampe, and Tesch-Römer (1993) proposed deliberate practice as a way to explain the genesis of expert performance, countering the popular belief that genetically endowed talent is behind it. According to their findings, experts engage in countless hours of a systematic practice—breaking down the elements of the skill or performance and, with each practice, carefully monitoring one's performance to identify errors, no matter how minute, in the elements. The next steps are to isolate the source of each error and to strive to correct it with each subsequent practice. Experts-to-be may work on only a couple of errors at a time, but they work their way through every one. Teachers or coaches usually enter the picture to help them find and correct errors. In addition, experts-to-be hold themselves to increasingly higher standards, aiming for mastery. Deliberate practice, then, revolves around finding and eliminating mistakes and doggedly pursing a moving target. It's hard, long, repetitive work—mentally demanding, emotionally straining, and life-engrossing. But deliberative practice goes far in explaining improvement and even exceptionality in performances in music (Duke, Simmons, & Cash, 2009), sports, and business, among other areas (Colvin, 2008).

Deliberate practice indeed incorporates self-regulated learning. While some people adopt deliberative practice with a grand goal in mind—performing at an extraordinarily brilliant level, typically in a career—others use it just to improve. However, the term usually applies to working on one specific (however complex) skill or performance, while self-regulated learning encompasses an interrelated web of skills, from reading different genres to writing various types of assignments to solving a wide range of problems.

Keeping deliberate practice in mind, however, you may notice more resemblances to self-regulated learning. People who practice either one of them seem to share beliefs about themselves, attitudes, and character traits.

Theoretical Roots of Self-Regulation

The concept of self-regulation emerged from Albert Bandura's seminal theory of self-efficacy (Zimmerman & Schunk, 2003), which was later incorporated into social cognition theory. While studying children, Bandura (1977, 1997) found that beliefs about their own self-efficacy seemed to determine how capably they thought they could self-regulate their thoughts and behavior. In turn, children with greater self-regulation were able to learn more, which in turn enhanced their sense of self-efficacy. These findings led Bandura (1986) to counsel K–12 educators to teach self-regulated learning in school. He recommended specifically that teachers focus on these three practices to foster students' self-efficacy and learning: first, their self-observation and self-monitoring of their performance; second, their self-evaluation of their performance against their personal standards and values, referential performances (models), and the determinants of performance; and third, their cognitive, affective, and tangible responses to their performance evaluations, including self-correction. Students with this kind of education would be less likely to buy into the notion of fixed intelligence (Dweck, 2007). For whatever reason, Bandura's recommendations did not transfer into educational practices, at least not as he intended them. The K–12 focus has been on cultivating student self-esteem rather than self-efficacy and self-regulation.

While self-efficacy and social cognition theory parented self-regulated learning, Zimmerman (2001) was able to reconcile self-regulated learning with the perspectives of six other prominent psychological theories: behaviorism, phenomenology, information processing, volition, Vygotsky, and constructivism. The neat fit of self-regulated learning with other theories enhances the validity of the concept as well as the research findings based on it. Full details appear in Zimmerman and Schunk (2001).

Self-regulated learning has also helped distinguish between novice and expert thinking. Drawing on the work of Schraw (1998), Bransford et al. (2000), and Zimmerman (2002), Grossman (2009) analyzed the very different perspectives that novices and experts take on their own learning. According to Grossman, novices tend to believe in an external locus of control and may give up on learning challenging material because they see their innate abilities as inadequate for the task. When they do choose to learn, novices go about it in a rather haphazard manner. They do not set goals or break up the task into steps or monitor their learning progress. They fail to evaluate and reorient their learning methods, if necessary. They rely on the feedback of others and compare their performance with others, rather than self-assessing and restructuring goals they have not met. In problem-solving situations, they rarely progress beyond exploring the problem (Schoenfeld, 2010). Experts, on the other hand, manage and control their learning all along, acknowledging failure as a signal to modify their learning strategies (Zimmerman, 2002). In problem solving, they read, explore, analyze, plan, implement their plans, and evaluate on their way to a solution (Schoenfeld, 2010).

Because self-regulated learning takes place over time—before, during, and after a learning session—Schraw (1998) developed a three-stage model of the process: planning, which precedes the learning task; monitoring, which goes on during it; and evaluating, which takes place immediately after it. At each stage, he posited, the self-regulated learner answers a *regulatory checklist* of questions, much like those that experts ask themselves while they are learning or problem solving. The following questions are representative.

- *Planning questions*: What kind of a task is this? What is my goal and how will I know I have reached it? How motivated am I to perform the task, and how can I increase my motivation if it's low? How much time and how many resources will be necessary? What do I already know about the topic? What additional information, if any, will I need? What strategies should I use? What strengths can I bring to the task? How can I compensate for my weaknesses? What might interfere with my completing the task, and how can I prevent this interference?
- *Monitoring questions*: Am I sure I know what I am doing? Does my approach to the task make sense? How well are my strategies working? Am I making good progress toward my goal? What changes in approach or strategies should I make, if any? What material is the most important? What material am I having trouble understanding? What material am I having trouble recalling? How does what I am learning relate to what I already know? How does it relate to my experience or my future? How is my thinking on the topic changing?
- *Evaluating questions*: How well did I achieve my goal? How well did I master what I set out to learn? How well did I avoid sources of interference and stay on task? What approach or strategy worked well? What didn't work? What do I need to do differently when taking on a similar task? What were the most important points I learned? What am I still having trouble understanding? What do I need to review? What questions do I have that should be answered by an expert? How does what I learned relate to other things I've been learning or have experienced? How has my thinking on the topic changed?

Zimmerman (1998, 2002) proposed a somewhat similar but more abstract framework of three "phases" of self-regulated learning: forethought, performance or volitional control, and self-reflection. Within each of these are two "classes" or classifications of more specific mental processes.

- Forethought
    - Class #1: Task analysis, to include goal setting and strategic planning
    - Class #2: Self-motivation beliefs, to include self-efficacy beliefs about one's learning, expectations about the personal consequences of learning (perceived value), intrinsic interest in the task (perceived value), and goal orientation (a learning orientation being better than a performance orientation)
- Performance/Volitional Control
    - Class #1: Self-control, to include use of imagery, self-instruction, attention focusing, and application of task strategies
    - Class #2: Self-observation, to include self-recording and self-experimenting (testing alternatives to see what works best)
- Self-Reflection
    - Class #1: Self-judgment, to include self-evaluation of one's apparent performance against some standard (one's prior performance, another person's performance, or some absolute standard) and one's causal attribution of results (beliefs about locus of control)
    - Class #2: Self-reaction, to include the degree of self-satisfaction, which enhances or undermines further motivation, and adaptive/defensive adjustments, which lead either to more effective learning strategies next time or to self-image protection, such as missing the test or dropping the course.

Schraw's and Zimmerman's schema both drive home the temporal nature of self-regulated learning. It is an ordered mental process—a sequenced *routine* practiced automatically by experts and seasoned learners.

Emotional Self-Regulation

Emotional control is an essential part of self-regulated learning, and Zimmerman's framework highlights this in two of his three phases. During forethought, the learner must motivate herself to tackle a learning task by consciously affirming her interest in doing it, its value to her, her sense of self-efficacy, and her desire for mastery. During the self-reflection that follows completing the task, she first judges her performance and then reacts emotionally to her judgment. Her being pleased reinforces her motivation and no doubt some of the other positive emotions she generated during forethought. Her being disappointed may lead to either her improving her learning strategies or her defensively withdrawing her energy from the task achievement goal. This last reaction may in turn undermine the positive emotions needed in the forethought phase of the next learning task.

The importance of positive feelings in the learning process cannot be overemphasized. No rational, mentally healthy person pursues a goal that defies one's reach or evokes negative affect toward oneself. But beyond this truism is a recently identified physiological link between emotions, cognitive acuity, and task performance (Immordino-Yang & Damasio, 2007; McCraty & Tomasino, 2006). For instance, research conducted on high-school students has found that high test anxiety, especially measures of worry, significantly depresses performance on high-stakes tests (Bradley et al., 2010). In this same study, the experimenters introduced an intervention called the TestEdge Program, in which the students in the treatment group successfully learned how to reduce their test anxiety and overall stress and how to generate positive emotions. In the matched-pairs analysis, these students achieved marginally significant higher test scores than those in the control group (Bradley et al., 2010). While the testing context is not directly relevant to self-regulated learning, this nascent line of research is pertinent to emotional self-regulation. The intervention program involves breathing slowly "through the heart," initiating thoughts that produce positive affect, and other mental exercises. Hopefully, the researchers will examine the effects of this simple intervention on learning. It could help break the indifferent, anxious, and defensive emotional attitudes that inhibit many students' learning process.

The Benefits of Self-Regulating Learning

As mentioned earlier, self-regulated learning is a sequenced series of practices that virtually any learner can understand and develop. It does not require any particular level of ability or intelligence (Schraw, 1998; Schraw & Dennison, 1994; Schunk & Zimmerman, 1998). Rather it takes, first, learning about the practices and their benefits, and then either wanting to implement these practices or responding positively to the external pressure to do so. For less internally motivated students, instructors can supply that pressure.

The payoffs for learners are significant and varied, although students may not believe it until they try out the strategies. Research has amassed overwhelming evidence that self-regulated learning enhances:

1. Student performance/achievement (learning) in courses and course units (Azevedo & Cromley, 2004; Boud, 1995, 2000; Cooper & Sandi-Urena, 2009; Garner & Alexander, 1989; Glenn, 2010; Hattie, 2009; Kitsantas & Zimmerman, 2009; Lovett, 2008; Masui & de Corte, 2005; McDonald & Boud, 2003; McGuire, 2008; Ottenhoff, 2011; Pintrich, 2002; Pressley & Ghatala, 1990; Rolf, Scharff, & Hodge, 2012; Schraw & Dennison, 1994; Zimmerman, 2002; Zimmerman, Moylan, Hudesman, White, & Flugman, 2011)
2. The amount and depth of student thinking (Jensen, 2011)
3. Students' conscious focus on their learning (Ottenhoff, 2011)
4. The development of reflective and responsible professionalism (Sluijsmans, Dochy, & Moerkerke, 1999)

In fact, the ability to self-regulate predicts SAT scores more strongly than does IQ, parental education, or parental economic status (Goleman, 1996).

Let's look at the relationship between learning and one mental process that plays prominently in self-regulated learning: self-assessment. It only makes sense that inaccurate self-assessment would be associated with poor self-regulation, but the former is also related to poor performance. In Kruger and Dunning's studies (1999, 2002), college students who ranked in the bottom quartile of the skills tested overestimated their rank by an average of 50 percentile points. Poor performance and inflated self-assessment of one's work were also linked in medical students (R. K. Edwards, Kellner, Sistrom, & Magyari, 2003) and undergraduates in other studies (Bell & Volckmann, 2011; Longhurst & Norton, 1997; Ottenhoff, 2011). One solution—having students develop their own grading criteria—proved ineffective. It failed to improve students' ability to discriminate levels of quality as well as the agreement between their grades and the grades given by the instructor and other students (Orsmond, Merry, & Reiling, 2000). The only silver lining here was some evidence that that poorer performers are less confident in their distorted self-estimations than are stronger performers in their more accurate self-estimations (Miller & Geraci, 2011).

Conversely, students who assess their work accurately—that is, the same way their instructor does—tend to be higher-achieving and more advanced (Boud & Falchikov, 1989, which is a broad literature review; R. K. Edwards et al., 2003), as well as more motivated (Longhurst & Norton, 1997). They are also more likely to be found in science courses (Falchikov & Boud, 1989) and mathematics courses like statistics (N. Edwards, 2007) than in other disciplines. Of course, this finding probably reflects the fact that, at the undergraduate level, scientific and mathematical problems usually have only one correct answer and limited ways of obtaining it.

Recall Bandura's findings that self-regulation and self-efficacy reinforce each other. As a result, the successful learner internalizes his locus of control and feels empowered to attribute successes and failures to his own study habits and efforts (Glenn, 2010; Masui & de Corte, 2005; Zimmerman, 2002; Zimmerman et al., 2011). Self-efficacy theory also tells us that a sense of control, choice, and volition enhances a person's motivation to perform a task. So, self-regulated learning, not surprisingly, is motivating in itself, even if the task is not particularly appealing to a learner. In a recent experimental study (Rolf et al., 2012), two groups of mathematics students were given preclass JiTT (Just-in-Time Teaching) homework assignments that required them to complete a reading and answer questions on it. The instructors then modified class activities based on students' responses. In the multiple-section treatment group, the instructors explained the learning benefits of the JiTT assignments and had the students complete three reflection forms on the effects of the JiTT process on their learning. The control group received neither the explanation not the reflective assignments. The results confirmed the positive impact of the metacognitive experiences—the instructors' explanations and students' reflections on their learning—on multiple facets of learning, including cognitive, affective, and motivational. The treatment-group students performed better on the final exam, expressed greater appreciation of the benefits of these assignments, and were more likely to answer the optional JiTT questions over the semester.

While Bandura (1977, 1997) linked self-regulation and self-discipline in children, no one has attempted to relate self-regulated learning to self-discipline in young adults. However, a connection is reasonable to expect. Self-regulation requires self-discipline, and vice versa. Self-regulation also contains elements of character and no doubt builds intellectual character. It fosters responsibility, introspective honesty, self-examination, and the pursuit of improvement. Schwartz and Sharpe (2012) had similar ideas in mind when the coined the term *intellectual virtues*, which include the love of truth, honesty, and perseverance among other positive traits. We can now better appreciate that developing self-regulated learning habits in our students is essential for higher education to realize its long-term goal of producing intentional, independent, self-directed, lifelong learners who can meet the burgeoning knowledge demands of the future.

Research tells us that one aspect of self-regulation, the ability to defer gratification while young, has profound effects on adult behavior and abilities. It fosters goal-setting, planning, self-esteem, ego resiliency, stress management, educational attainment, and social and cognitive competency (Mischel & Ayduk, 2002; Mischel, Shoda, & Peake, 1988; Mischel, Shoda, & Rodriguez, 1989; Shoda, Mischel, & Peake, 1990), as well as income attainment (Evans & Rosenbaum, 2008).

The Structure of This Book

The next eight chapters comprise a catalog of activities and assignments in which students self-regulate their learning—to include cognitive processes, emotions, motivations, behavior, and environment—around different course components and on various schedules. These include metacognitive assignments, which I call *meta-assignments*, in which students monitor and document their own thinking and actions in completing content-based assignments. Elliott (2010) coined the term *meta-assignment* as a means to help the millennial ("trophy") generation develop sharper "intellectual clarity."

Along the way, you will also come across the term *wrappers*, which Lovett (2008) conceived to designate activities and assignments that direct students' attention to self-regulation before, during, or after regular course components. As the word suggests, they wrap around assigned readings, videos, podcasts, lectures, regular course assignments, quizzes, and exams. Their purpose is to heighten students' conscious awareness of their learning process: what they are and are not understanding or retaining, how they are or are not learning, what they are deeming important, how they are tackling and proceeding with an assignment, how they are processing and responding to a learning experience, how well they are executing and realizing their plans and goals, what value they are obtaining from a learning task, how much they are progressing on a given skill, how much confidence they have in their knowledge and skills, how much they may be overestimating their knowledge and skills, and how effectively and diligently they are preparing for quizzes and exams. Wrappers not only enhance students' performance on the regular course components but also teach them how their mind works and how to make it learn and perform better. In doing so, wrappers multiply the learning value of every standard class activity and assignment.

We know that students, even at the elementary level, acquire self-regulated learning strategies by witnessing others modeling these techniques—whether the modeling is being done by the instructor (Butler & Winne, 1995) or student peers (Schunk, 1989)—and then by practicing them on their own (R. Brown & Pressley, 1994; Delclos & Harrington, 1991; Kuhn, Schauble, & Garcia-Mila, 1992; Schraw, 1998; Schraw & Dennison, 1994; Siegler & Jenkins, 1989). So observing a model "talking out" a self-regulatory process may be the first stage of skill acquisition for students, but they must then engage in activities or assignments to develop their nascent skills. To the extent possible, these tasks should be worth something toward the course grade. Giving credit drives home to students the importance we give to learning how to learn, and it need not take more than a few minutes of our time. But we delay issues of credit and grading until chapter 10.

In chapter 11 we consider ways to integrate self-regulated learning into course design. This integration, which should be evident in the syllabus, communicates to students that learning how to learn is a worthy, if not critical, learning outcome in itself. Actually, this outcome is a package of outcomes focusing on different aspects of the self-regulation process. After addressing the objections that faculty may raise to this integration, the chapter offers recommendations on which assignments and activities to incorporate first. Those suggested demand little or no class time and grading time but have a major impact on student achievement. Hopefully, they can give instructors the confidence to add a few more easy-to-implement self-regulated activities and assignments over the next couple of times that they teach a course, and some early additions are suggested. One option for achieving a fully integrated course is to have students assemble a learning portfolio that includes all of their self-regulated learning products as well as their content- and skills-related work. Chapter 5 examines different types of portfolios as meta-assignments.

The final chapter offers models for integrated course design. It describes a number of disparate courses—from several in scientific, technical/engineering, and mathematical (STEM) fields to developmental writing—that explicitly feature self-regulated learning outcomes in parallel to knowledge and skill outcomes. In a couple of these courses, students build a sizable portfolio of their self-regulatory reflections and wrappers over the term. Other courses have been the subjects of rigorous research on the impact of self-regulated learning activities and assignments on student achievement. The findings document that many and often most students make impressive leaps in learning the subject matter, problem solving, and writing skills when they are practicing self-regulated learning in tandem. In addition, a few studies show that struggling students benefit the most from learning self-regulation (Ottenhoff, 2011). So why shouldn't we weave it into our regular content-related outcomes?

This book is best seen not just as a catalog of exercises and activities to use here and there for spicing up your course. Rather, consider it as a guide to structuring a course that teaches not only disciplinary knowledge and skills but also proven strategies to learn and retain them, for your course and long beyond it. Every instructor and every course has the time to provide self-regulated learning opportunities because they need not entail much time in or out of class, for us or our students. Rather than take away from the content, they help students learn it.

2

FOSTERING SELF-REGULATED LEARNING FROM THE START

I f you are going to showcase self-regulated learning among your student learning outcomes, you should start your course with one or more activities or assignments to prime your students for this emphasis. But even if not, you may want to use some of the options described in this chapter in your class. Be aware that none of them is a wrapper, as described in chapter 1, and most of them are independent of other coursework and the content. Still, some faculty, including those in the sciences, have incorporated even content-extraneous activities and assignments into their courses because they know their students will do higher-quality work and learn the material better as a result (e.g., see Perkins, 2008; Wirth, 2008a; 2008b).

The self-assessment activities described in the last two sections of this chapter can and usually should be repeated at least at the end of the course so that students can see how much they have learned. Of course, you, too, can see how much they have learned, and you might want to use your results as evidence of student learning to submit in your faculty reviews.

Readings and Discussions on Learning and Thinking

Few students have ever read anything about the nature of learning or thinking, so one assignment you might give during the first week of a course is a short, student-oriented reading on what learning entails. Fortunately, at least two excellent alternatives are available for free on the web:

Learning (Your First Job), by Robert Leamnson (2002) at www.udel.edu/CIS/106/iaydin/07F/misc/firstJob.pdf—In this 12-page essay, Leamnson addresses a wide variety of cognitive topics: the brain biology of learning, the difference between *understanding* and *remembering*, how to listen actively to a lecture and take notes, how to develop an interest in a subject, how to use out-of-class time productively, the difference between *knowledge* and *information* and how to use the former to make sense out of the latter, and how to prepare for and take exams. He gives wise, research-based advice on how to study and effectively drives home the point that learning involves work and effort for all students but can be very rewarding.

"Learning to Learn," by Karl R. Wirth and Dexter Perkins (2008b) at http://www.macalester.edu/academics/geology/wirth/learning.pdf—This 29-page manuscript is longer and more advanced than Leamnson's, summarizing many of the schema that faculty learn in the course of their own professional development. However, Perkins (2008) and Wirth (2008a; 2008b) both regularly assign it to their geology undergraduates, suggesting that, with some effort, students can understand it. The major topics are the failure of traditional teaching; the shift from teaching to learning; the student learning needs for the twenty-first century; thinking and learning in the cognitive, affective, and psychomotor domains; Fink's (2003) categories of significant learning; Kolb's (1984) learning cycle; the changes in the brain associated with learning; Perry's (1968) stages of intellectual development; Baxter Magolda's (1992) levels of intellectual development; Paul and Elder's (2011) elements of critical thinking; metacognition; Soloman and Felder's (n.d.) learning style dimensions; the behavioral dimensions of grades; and the contrasting characteristics of successful, average, and struggling students.

If you assign this kind of reading, you need to leave time for in-class discussion the date it is due. You thus need a "discussion-size" class, perhaps one under 40 people, in which many students will feel free to speak up. The discussion may start out with some recall (recitation) questions that warm up students' minds to the material, but a good discussion is an exchange of experiences and viewpoints, so it relies on your asking questions with multiple correct answers (Nilson, 2010). You might pose questions like these to your class:

- What was the most important insight you gained from the reading?
- What surprised you most in the reading?
- What did you already know?
- Did you identify with any of Kolb's learning styles? Which one or ones?
- Which one of Perry's stages of intellectual development did you identify with?
- One of Fink's categories of significant learning is learning how to learn, the subject we're addressing in this class right now. Have you been taught how to learn before? Where? What did you learn about learning?

- What will you do differently during a lecture, if anything, given what you read?
- How will you prepare differently for exams, given what you read?
- Can you think of other good learning practices that the reading didn't mention?

This kind of open-ended question reduces the fear of public speaking. As long as a student is trying to contribute to the discussion in good faith, giving a wrong answer is almost impossible.

If your class is too large for a discussion or is online, you can turn some of the open-ended questions into reflective homework questions for your students to answer in writing. Taking this approach ensures that students read the article and apply its advice to improve their own learning.

While students can learn a great deal about self-regulated learning exploring either of these readings, bear in mind that neither one has any link to course content, requiring that you carve out homework time as well as class time for it.

Goal Setting

Because setting a goal is the first thing a self-regulated learner does when taking on a learning or problem-solving task, having your students set positive goals for your course prepares them for later self-regulating practices. Perkins (2008) has his students write answers to the questions, "Why are you in this class? What are your goals?" This exercise can be a brief, informal, in-class writing assignment that can go on paper, on getting-to-know-you index cards, or online. It can also serve as a launch pad for an icebreaking activity, a small-group exchange, or a brief class discussion.

Another goal-setting activity suitable for class or homework is to have your students write a paper titled "How I Earned an A in This Course," dated the *last* day of the semester (after final exams). Zander and Zander (2000) devised this interesting exercise in optimism and commitment as a transformative activity to elevate students' ambitions and make them more concrete and attainable. Self-regulated learning proponents such as Perkins (2008) and Wirth (2008a), among others, have adopted it for their classes. Not only does it help students set a high goal for themselves, but it also induces them to develop plans for attaining that goal. While students used to earning As may simply summarize their successful strategies for reading, studying, project planning, writing, and test taking, lower-achieving students have to give the paper some genuine thought, maybe even a bit of research. One good source may be the last section of Wirth and Perkins

(2008b), where the authors contrast what successful, average, and struggling students do. These less-than-A students must consider why and where their performance has been coming up short and how to correct and improve their strategies. Self-assessment like this, followed by planning more effective means to achieve the goal, constitutes the heart of self-regulated learning. This assignment suggests possible follow-up activities such as a class or small-group discussion on what it takes to get an A or an end-of-course follow-up paper titled either "How I Actually Earned an A in This Course" or "Why I Didn't Earn an A in This Course."

Alternatively, you can replace this paper with an in-class exercise in which student groups brainstorm ways to earn an A in your course and share these ideas with the class to evaluate. You can then record the better strategies to display all semester either online or in your classroom on a large piece of paper (L. Sager, personal communication, March 16, 2012). In a distance learning course, groups can brainstorm in their chat space and post their final list of strategies on the class discussion board.

As useful as such goal-setting assignments and activities can be, they are removed from the course content and require allocating homework time for the paper(s) or class time for idea generation or follow-up discussion.

Self-Assessment of Self-Regulated Learning Skills

Having your students fill out an instrument that assesses their self-regulated learning skills, presumably at the beginning and the end of your course, makes sense only if you intend to include self-regulation among your learning outcomes and commit considerable time to helping your students develop it. Two validated instruments are available for this purpose; a third option leads students through an open-ended set of questions.

The first, designed by Cooper and Sandi-Urena (2009), is the 27-item Metacognitive Activities Inventory (MCAI). While these researchers created it for chemistry students, it can measure metacognitive problem-solving skills in other STEM areas as well. The complete instrument is at http://pubs.acs .org/doi/abs/10.1021/ed086p240, but here are a few sample items:

- When I do assigned problems, I try to learn more about the concepts so that I can apply this knowledge to test problems.
- Once a result is obtained, I check to see that it agrees with what I expected.
- I jot down things that I know might help me solve a problem before attempting a solution.
- I start solving problems without having to read all the details of the statement. (Cooper & Sandi-Urena, 2009, p. 242)

Note that the last item is phrased in reverse, as are several other items; agreeing indicates a lack of a metacognitive skill.

The second instrument, called the Metacognitive Awareness Inventory, assesses general self-regulated learning skills across the disciplines. Developed by Schraw and Dennison (1994), it has 52 items classified by type of cognitive knowledge—declarative (DK), procedural (PK), and conditional (CK)—or by specific metacognitive process—planning (P), information management strategies (IMS), monitoring (M), debugging strategies (DS), and evaluation (E). The following are eight sample items, each representing a different classification:

- I have control over how well I learn. DK
- I am aware of what strategies I use when I study. PK
- I use my intellectual strengths to compensate for my weaknesses. CK
- I think about what I really need to learn before I begin a task. P
- I consider several alternatives to a problem before I answer. M
- I summarize what I've learned after I finish. E
- I draw pictures or diagrams to help me understand while learning. IMS
- I change strategies when I fail to understand. DS (Schraw & Dennison, 1994, pp. 473–474)

This being such a long instrument, you might want to select 15 or 30 self-assessment items for your students that target the skills on which you plan your course to focus the most. But you can also look at this instrument as an excellent list of metacognitive skills, one that you might want to distribute to and discuss with your students.

The third option is a set of web pages that poses open-ended questions to help students find out how they learn and how they might learn more effectively, particularly with respect to reading. Landsberger (1996–2012) designed it as part of the online Study Guides and Strategies series; it is part self-assessment and part advice on learning how to learn. Some of the questions echo those in Schraw's (1998) three-stage model of the self-regulatory process. They are grouped in sets of four steps, the first of which is unconnected to the course content, but the questions in Steps 2, 3, and 4 pertain to a specific reading assignment. Thus, they can serve as occasional reading wrappers (see chapter 3 for more), starting with the first reading as a baseline and ending with the last reading to record the student's progress toward becoming self-regulating.

The first set of questions explores a student's past experience as a learner: what he enjoyed learning, how he studied, how he learned to study, and how he liked to show his learning. The second set focuses on a current reading task, specifically the student's interest, focus, environment, and plan. The third group represents what a self-regulated learner would ask himself when starting the task to ascertain his initial understanding, recall his prior knowledge, and determine his resource needs. Finally, the last set leads the learner through a self-evaluation of his strategic choices and self-discipline. The list of all the questions is available at www.studygs.net/meta cognitiona, but students should complete the exercises at www.studygs.net/ metacognition and print them out. Landsberger invites students to improve their metacognitive skills by using the wide variety of available study guides and strategies that are all just a click away.

Of course, these self-assessment instruments should not be graded and should be used only to help students appraise their progress toward becoming self-regulated learners.

Self-Assessment on Course Knowledge and Skills

This type of student self-assessment incorporates the course content—the knowledge and the skills—that you plan for your students to acquire. Such self-assessment is designed to be done twice: once at the beginning of the course and again at the end. The first self-assessment is diagnostic, but it serves other instructional purposes as well: activating students' prior knowledge of the content to prepare them for adding new knowledge; revealing student misconceptions about the subject matter, so that you can address and dispel them head-on during the course; and previewing the learning that is to come, even if students do not fully understand the vocabulary, processes, or problem-solving techniques. The first self-assessment exercise should not be scored or graded. The second one makes students aware of all that they have gained in the interim, so that they cannot leave the course thinking that they haven't learned anything, which some occasionally claim. This second run-through is often graded.

Reflective Writing

Scholars of teaching and assessment have developed and used many forms of student self-assessment on course content. The simplest is to have students write a brief reflection in class or as homework on the nature of the subject matter of the course and its importance—for example, "What is history (or biology or philosophy or mathematics)? Why is this subject important?" (Suskie, 2004). These specific questions are most appropriate in an introductory course. While these first answers may be flawed, students should generate much more sophisticated ones at the end of the course, which you can grade if you choose.

Kraft (2008) devised a somewhat more elaborate and more structured option to help her geoscience students understand science and scientific thinking in general, as well as their own habits of mind. They respond to these prompts: "What is the nature of science? How is science done? What examples does geology provide?" Students could just write out their answers, but at the beginning of the course, Kraft distributes sets of cards with statements about science, some accurate and others inaccurate (from Cobern & Loving, 1998) to answer the first two questions. Students choose the cards that represent their view of science, first on their own and then in a small group, and the group must concur on their card selections. At the end of the course, the same small groups reconvene to author a collective statement about the nature of science, how it is conducted, and how geology illustrates the scientific method. In addition, individual students write reflections on how and why their conceptions of science have changed, as well as how their answers to the prompts may differ from their group's. According to Kraft, her students always demonstrate the most metacognitive thinking when they reflect on how their ideas about science have changed. These individual writings may be graded but need not be.

Content-Focused Writing

Content-focused writing can—and in the two examples given here do—furnish the basis for the final exam. In her version, Griffiths (2010) gives her students an ungraded writing assignment to answer a series of essay questions. Since she teaches criminology, her questions ask students to do things such as define *miscarriage of justice*, distinguish it from *wrongful conviction*, estimate the incidence of such occurrences, and state the main causes. Griffiths collects these first assignments and returns them to the students at the end of the course when she distributes the final exam. For the final, students take the role of a new criminology instructor with a PhD and write a critique of their first assignment, correcting inaccuracies, identifying misconceptions, pointing out errors in reasoning, and supplying a more complete and correct response to each question.

If you would like to try Griffiths's assessment method, you can follow her model and devise questions on key concepts, principles, techniques, processes, important statistics, causes, effects, and the like. However, these tap mainly into factual knowledge and information from the course materials. Feel free to develop more thought-provoking questions that the readings and classroom activities do not answer directly, such as asking students to venture an explanation of a paradoxical phenomenon or to take and defend one side or the other of a debate.

Another version of content-focused writing that has students self-assessing their course knowledge and skills was developed by Clemson University professor of anthropology Michael Coggeshall (personal correspondence, 2010–11). His procedure starts with a first-week, ungraded writing assignment that he calls a *perspective assessment survey*. He gives his students seven anthropological propositions—most false, but some true—and asks them to take a stand on each one: strongly agree, agree, not sure, disagree, or strongly disagree. Then they must justify their position in a sentence or two. Coggeshall recommends that students complete the assignment in eight to 10 minutes. The statements include, "Plant/animal domestication represented a major improvement in human social history; most human lives drastically improved afterward." "Native peoples of North America (north of Mexico) never developed any complex societies until Europeans arrived." "Ideas about God and/or the supernatural (including your own) are not 'revealed' but 'created' by social leaders to fulfill major social and psychological needs." For the final exam, Coggeshall returns these first-week assignments and has his students critique and rewrite four of their original seven responses, incorporating supporting evidence and explaining how their thinking has changed. (Their choice of propositions is limited, and these essays are much longer than the first-week responses.) He does not grade students on whether they change their position but rather on how well they are able to justify their current position with evidence. This criterion reflects his most important student learning outcome. He also uses the summary results of his "value-added essay final" as a measure of his students' learning for submission in his faculty reviews.

To implement Coggeshall's strategy, first recall some commonly held myths that most students coming into your course consider to be true but that your field has overturned. Often these myths are serious misconceptions you need to be aware of and address explicitly during the course.

Knowledge Surveys

Knowledge surveys are questionnaires that ask students to rate their confidence in their ability to answer questions and perform tasks that a course will address or has already addressed (Nuhfer, 1996; Nuhfer & Knipp, 2003; Wirth & Perkins, 2008a). These questions and tasks should collectively encompass the important content and skills of an entire course or course unit. Students can respond to each item in seconds, so they should be able to complete a 200-item survey in 20 to 30 minutes (Wirth & Perkins, 2008a). Of course, you have to tailor knowledge surveys to your specific courses, but you can glean items from your learning outcomes, homework assignments, in-class exercises, old exams, and even new exams that you plan to give later the same term. In this way, you ensure that your students read your learning outcomes for them, and you make the relationship between content and assessment more transparent. If students have little understanding of a question or task, they are not likely to remember it. But even if they do, there is no problem in their remembering what they have learned in your course that is important. In fact, it is a plus. Wirth and Perkins (2008a) even recommend that students retain their first knowledge survey and use the document during the course to alert them to important material and to serve as study guides.

According to Wirth and Perkins (2008a), the content and skills represented in a knowledge survey should cover a broad, if not the full, spectrum of Bloom's (1956) hierarchy of cognitive operations or L. W. Anderson and Krathwohl's (2000) updated version of the taxonomy. The following are examples of questions and tasks at each of the six levels of thinking:

- Name and define the various dissociative disorders. (knowledge/ remembering)
- What argument is Socrates making in this passage from his *Apology*? (comprehension/understanding)
- Apply Archimedes' Principle to measure the volume of this irregularly shaped object. (application/applying)
- In these drug trials, what variables must be controlled? (analysis/ analyzing)
- Script a lesson to explain electromagnetism to a 12-year-old. (synthesis/ creating)
- Assess the investments in this portfolio for the objective of (a) aggressive growth, (b) growth, (c) income. (evaluation/evaluating)

Of course, the levels of the cognitive operations that a given knowledge survey should represent depends on the course.

The survey directions should instruct students to rate their confidence level in their ability to answer the questions or perform the tasks and *explicitly* tell them *not* to answer the questions or perform the tasks. You can simply list levels of confidence—such as (a) Very confident, (b) Somewhat confident, (c) Not sure, and (d) Not at all confident—or you can design more elaborate answers, like the following (adapted from Wirth & Perkins, 2005):

- I do not understand the question or task, or I do not understand the technical terms, or I do not think I can give a correct answer.
- I think I understand the question and (a) I think I can answer at least half of it correctly, or (b) I know exactly where to find the information I need to give a correct answer in 20 minutes or less.
- I know that I can answer the question well enough for grading now.

The last option can be broken down into two, one in which the student believes her answer would get a passing grade but no higher, and another option in which she believes her answer would get a very good grade. Since so many students are so savvy about locating information on the Internet, you might want to reduce to time limit from 20 minutes to one or two minutes.

Because knowledge surveys tap into student perceptions, the answers often distort reality. Students do not always know what they do and do not know. Specifically, they tend to *over*estimate their knowledge and abilities, except possibly the best students, and the gap between what they know and what they *think* they know widens among the poorly performing students (Bell & Volckmann, 2011; Kruger & Dunning, 1999, 2002; Longhurst & Norton, 1997; Miller & Geraci, 2011). Despite this inflation effect, the results of knowledge surveys do vary with actual knowledge, and they can be used to measure student learning at the course level (Wirth & Perkins, 2008a).

The major benefit for students comes at the end of the course when they fill out the same knowledge survey they took at the beginning and can compare their then-and-now answers side by side. As with the before-and-after writing assignments described previously under "Self-Assessment on Course Knowledge and Skills," knowledge surveys help students realize all the new content and skills they have learned in your course. Their awareness enhances their confidence and self-efficacy as learners, which in turn fosters their self-regulation.

Laying the Foundation

As we all know, the first day of class sets the tone for the term, and introducing self-regulated learning as soon as possible, certainly within the first day or two of class, is important. It should first appear in the syllabus as one or more student learning outcomes. If you plan to have your students develop a course learning portfolio, your earliest self-regulated learning assignment or writing activity will be their first entry, serving as a baseline measure of their current content knowledge and skills (real or perceived) or their first informed understanding of learning.

To whatever degree you bring self-regulated learning into your courses, be sure to share your intentions with your students from the beginning. Explain to them what self-regulated learning is and how it can benefit them and their content learning. Tell them how certain assignments and activities will help them develop their skills, and then remind them during the term. Pintrich (2002) recommends this kind of explicit treatment of the subject. In this way, your students will better understand and appreciate all that you are doing for them.

3

SELF-REGULATED READING, WATCHING, AND LISTENING

Not many students know how to learn from their readings. In general, students rarely interact with the text; ask questions; evaluate the source; anticipate what will come next; or connect what they are reading with their lives, emotions, and what they already know (Bean, 2011). They are used to looking only for facts and terms, which are usually not the most important parts of the message, and often misinterpret concepts and ideas to fit their own preconceived notions, rather than reexamine their own beliefs and schema. In addition, they don't know how to adapt their reading strategies to different genres, and they underestimate the time and effort required for deep reading (Bean, 2011). Since a great deal of lifelong learning relies on reading, we need to help our students strengthen their reading comprehension, efficiency, persistence, and retention. This chapter offers a variety of methods to help them make more of their reading. Many of these methods also increase the likelihood that students will do the readings that you assign by holding them accountable and modestly rewarding their compliance (Nilson, 2010; Ottenhoff, 2011).

Because many students struggle with reading, they may prefer getting their knowledge from other media, which is why some scholars urge faculty to "flip their classroom" by replacing as many readings and live lectures as possible with video- and audio-recorded presentations for homework (Bergmann & Sams, 2012; Bowen, 2012). Whether produced by the instructor or someone else, these presentations should be online and relatively brief. Then, proponents maintain, students will be ready for a face-to-face class meeting full of activities on that knowledge. Students may very well be more amenable to watching a 15-minute YouTube clip and listening to a 10-minute podcast than reading a 30-page chapter. However, a person can watch and listen to anything without planning, monitoring, and evaluating learning. Therefore, within a few limits, the same self-regulated learning assignments that enhance reading should apply to homework that is listened to or viewed. Such assignments also help ensure that students actually do this homework.

Virtually all the assignments in this chapter were developed to accompany readings because the flipped classroom concept is quite new. However, I extrapolate their applicability to homework in other media wherever possible.

Reflective Writing

Reflective writing aims to make students aware of how they are metacognitively processing and reacting to the readings, videos, or podcasts. It directs them to focus on (a) how effectively they are learning from the homework, given their approach, and (b) how they are integrating the content into their current cognitive and affective schema. In other words, it induces them to *observe themselves* before, during, and after their reading, watching, or listening experience. Reflective writing differs from "genre content questions," which the next section addresses, in that the latter direct students to analyze and find specific points in the content.

Within the myriad of reflective writing prompts available in the literature, you may find a few that fit your needs perfectly. But if not, let what others have found useful inspire you to compose your own.

Recall from the last chapter Landsberger's (1996–2012) web pages of open-ended questions probing students about how they learn and how they might learn more effectively (www.studygs.net/metacognition). The questions in Steps 2, 3, and 4 pertain to a specific reading, video, or podcast assignment. Step 2 addresses the student's interest, focus, environment, and plan; Step 3, his initial understanding, recall of prior knowledge, and resource needs; and Step 4, a self-evaluation of his strategic choices and self-discipline. Therefore, if you have your students answer these questions with every homework assignment or at least some of them, each student's set of responses will constitute a record of his progress toward becoming more self-regulating. He can also learn how to improve his metacognitive skills by clicking on links to various study guides and strategies.

The Study Cycle, developed at the Center for Academic Success at Louisiana State University (2010) and promoted by McGuire (2008), similarly leads students through a learning process that culminates in self-regulation. First, they should preview the readings before class (skim, read summaries, etc.). This first step is not transferable to videos and podcasts. Then students should attend class; review their notes from the class within 24 hours; ask themselves why, how, and what-if questions; and finally assess their learning on a regular basis. In addition, they should periodically evaluate the effectiveness of their study methods and test themselves on their ability to teach the material to others. For these last two tasks, the website gives students good reflective writing prompts to assess their approach to and understanding of their homework.

Kalman (2007) introduced a reflective writing exercise to help his students read and comprehend each chapter of a physics textbook, but you can adapt it to almost any challenging reading, video, or podcast. His exercise directs students to pinpoint the most important concepts and principles and identify what they don't understand clearly. After reading a section or two of the chapter and highlighting or underlining the critical phrases and passages, students free-write about the reading for approximately two-thirds of a page, with the emphasis on what the reading *means*, then about what they have questions about and don't understand. The two free-writing tasks encourage different facets of self-regulated learning. The first serves a self-testing function by making students aware of what they can (and cannot) recall and how they make sense of it, while the second directs their attention to what they are not grasping and need to clarify in class. Because students wind up doing so many free-writes over the term, Kalman counts them in total as 20% of the course grade, but he evaluates them only on completeness. In his research on this exercise, Kalman has found that students learn the material better and perform better on tests. While students may not like the extra work, they do acknowledge by mid-semester that it helps them master physics.

Another strategy to encourage students to self-regulate their reading—or their viewing or listening—is to require that they observe and jot down their affective and other personal reactions to the material (Bean, 2011). Their record can take the form of marginalia or double-column notes—one column for substantive notes and the other for reactions. Of course, monitoring the students' compliance with double-column notes is easier if you collect them at least occasionally. The reactions that students record may tap into their feelings, attitudes, values, beliefs, perspectives, past experiences, prior knowledge, or changes in their way of thinking. This exercise not only encourages students to focus on the reading, video, or podcast and reflect on its personal meaning but also makes them associate the material with emotions, strengthening their delicate new synaptic connections (Zull, 2011).

A minute paper, which is a particularly popular end-of-class-period classroom assessment technique (CAT), can serve as a reading, video, or podcast wrapper to foster self-regulated learning. You can have your students respond to any number of prompts that sensitize them to their experiences with the homework. The following are just a few ideas that students can ponder and write about immediately after completing a reading, video, or podcast (adapted from Angelo & Cross, 1993; Wirth, 2008a; Wirth, n.d.):

- The most important point of the reading, video, or podcast
- The most useful or valuable thing(s) they learned
- The most surprising or unexpected ideas
- What ideas stand out in their mind
- What helped or hindered their understanding of the reading, video, or podcast
- The most confusing points, and why they were confusing
- What idea(s) they can and should put into practice immediately
- How they would paraphrase the key content for a high school student
- How the material connects with or breaks from their prior knowledge
- How it connects with their knowledge from other courses
- How it fits into their existing framework of knowledge (Mezeske, 2009)

Wirth (n.d.) routinely has his students write reading reflections to three of the previous prompts: What is the main point? What did they find most surprising? What did they find most confusing, and why did they find it confusing? While these questions look simple, Wirth (2008a) has found that these reflections correlate with final course grades more strongly than any other of the many self-regulated learning activities and assignments he weaves through his courses. Specifically, the more faithfully and thoughtfully students complete this assignment, the better they perform in the course. Naturally, these reflections motivate students to do the readings to begin with, but the readings are not the only source of tested content and skills. The correlation between students' reading reflections and their grade has been a startling .86, and, by extrapolation, these reflections have accounted for 74% of the variance in the course grades (slide 31). Following the JiTT (Just-in-TimeTeaching) method, Wirth collects his students' reading reflections online and uses them to shape his lecture and activities for the next class meeting.

Genre Content Questions

Genre content questions call less for reflection than for cognitive analysis of the content. For this reason, they serve more to instruct students on how to read, watch, or listen to a given piece or whole genre of work—what to look for and how to identify the crucial components. In other words, they teach students an analytic strategy. Sets of standard questions are already available for several genres and are summarized later. But if you prefer or have to compose your own questions, your goal is to develop a set that you can assign repeatedly for a given genre. Genres in reading, for example, include a novel, a point-of-view essay or book, a scientific journal article, or a textbook. The videos and podcasts you assign in your classes may also fall into different genres.

For instance, if your students are reading a novel, your questions would direct students to conduct a basic literary analysis—pick out major characters, note their salient traits and critical interactions, describe the writing style, trace the plot, identify uses of literary devices such as symbolism and foreshadowing, uncover more general social messages, and the like.

For a point-of-view essay or book, you would pose questions like these: What is the author's central thesis or claim? What motivated the author to make this claim? To what is the author reacting? What is the organization or structure of the author's argument—that is, what are the major points made in support of the thesis or claim? What evidence does the author provide to back up each of these points? What points can you argue against using different evidence? Of course, you may want to add some reflective questions as well, such as, how did your mind change, if at all, while reading the work? Also, by the end, how persuasive did you find the author's argument and evidence?

Scientific journal articles require a different kind of analysis, a kind that one team of scholars called a "self-regulated thematic set of questions" (Rose et al., 2008). This set includes points that we automatically look for ourselves when we are reading research in our discipline. Students, of course, must learn to ask and find answers to these questions: Why did the authors conduct this research? What issues or unknowns in the literature motivated them? How did they develop their hypotheses or research questions? What constitute their data, and how did they collect them? Why did they choose the data analysis techniques they did? What conclusions did they draw from their data? To what extent were these conclusions warranted? What limitations of the study did they note? What limitations, if any, did they miss? What is the significance of their findings? What does their study contribute to the field?

A textbook is a genre unto its own, and questions at the end of each chapter often draw attention to the concepts, principles, and phenomena that you want your students to be able to recognize, describe, explain, or apply. If not, you may want to add questions like these: What are the most important points, central concepts, or key principles in the chapter? How is this chapter related to the previous chapter? How is it related to its larger section of the textbook? How is concept X related to concept Y? How do concepts X and Y differ? What are three examples of concept X (or principle X) not already given in the textbook? How can you apply material in the chapter to solve a problem or accomplish a task?

A final type of genre content question is the kind you have your students compose themselves for a future quiz or exam. When you have them generate test questions from the readings, videos, or podcasts, you and the students both realize several benefits. First, they learn to identify what is important. Second, they self-test their own understanding of the material, because writing good exam questions on content you don't understand is almost impossible. In addition, you save yourself time and effort now in putting tests together and later in dealing with students who might complain about test questions. After all, if you didn't write the questions, they have no argument with you.

For this assignment to work well, you have to teach your students how to write well-constructed, thought-provoking test items. You might familiarize them with Bloom's (1956) or L. W. Anderson and Krathwohl's (2000) taxonomy of cognitive operations and give students credit for only higher-order thinking questions (application, analysis, synthesis, and evaluation). Just teaching them about different levels of thinking adds to their metacognitive skills. They also have to learn how to structure different types of items properly (true-false, multiple-choice, multiple true-false, completion, essay), and plenty of sources are available to help you and them in this task (e.g., Gronlund & Waugh, 2009; Jacobs & Chase, 1992; Nilson, 2010; Ory & Ryan, 1993; Suskie, 2004).

Self-Testing of Recall

All serious books and websites on study skills recommend essentially the same reading procedure. SQ3R, for instance, expands to survey, question, read, recall, review, and PQR3 stands for preview, question, read, recite, review. To *survey* or *preview* a reading means to thumb through it first, finding what it is about and how it is organized, usually by looking at the headings, subheadings, and any italicized or bolded words. The *question* part directs students to give themselves a purpose for their reading by developing questions to answer from the headings and subheadings. This recommendation presumes that the instructor is not supplying reflective, critical reading, or study questions to guide their reading. But to improve your students' self-regulated learning skills, you may very well be supplying questions that tell them what they should be investigating. In the *read* stage, students should be reading the assigned pages purposively with an eye toward answering those questions.

The fourth and fifth parts of the procedure foster the development of students' self-regulated learning skills, as well longer-term content learning. After reading, a student should put away the book and notes and recall all she can, either reciting aloud or writing down everything she can remember. Then she should go back and review the reading, looking for whatever important points she forgot or recalled incorrectly. This technique has considerable research supporting its effectiveness. For example, Roediger and Karpicke (2006) found that rereading fact-based material again and again (specifically 14 times on average) resulted in substantially lower recall a week later than reading and reproducing the material just a few times (specifically 3.4 times on average). In fact, using the recall-and-review method proved to be just as effective as note taking, which requires more time, for short-term and delayed free recall of fact-based material (McDaniel, Howard, & Einstein, 2009). And unlike note taking, recall-and-review gives the learner the benefits of getting immediate feedback on how well she processed the reading as well as retrieval practice and rehearsal (McDaniel et al., 2009; Roediger & Karpicke, 2006).

While students may not be able to survey or preview a video or podcast nor make up questions from subheadings, you can supply study questions to give them a purpose for viewing or listening. In addition, they can practice recalling the content and replay the video or podcast to find any important points that they missed or remembered incorrectly.

Recent literature reviews (Roediger & Butler, 2010; Roediger & Karpicke, 2006) allude to dozens of studies confirming the learning principle called the "testing effect," which is the product of retrieval practice, feedback, and repetition. Self-regulated learning calls for self-testing (self-evaluation) and provides retrieval practice, self-feedback, and review. Repeated self-testing is the principle behind flash cards and Total Recall Learning (TRL), which itself is based on flash cards and used in corporate, hospital, and military training. Designed to counter the "curve of forgetting" proposed by Hermann Ebbinghaus (S. F. Davis & Palladino, 2002; Fuchs, 1997), TRL claims to realize knowledge retention of over 90%.

While just one element of repeated self-testing, retrieval practice has attracted considerable research. It serves to familiarize the mind with new material quickly and to reduce cognitive load with each retrieval. As a result, the mind can think *about* the material, realizing deep learning and conceptual understanding, which in turn allows more flexible retrieval and easier transfer of the material to new situations (Butler, 2010; C. I. Johnson & Mayer, 2009; McDaniel et al., 2009; Rohrer, Taylor, & Sholar, 2010).

Even though our interest is self-regulated learning, frequent quizzes administered by the instructor have the same effect as self-testing (Bangert-Drowns, Kulik, Kulik, & Morgan, 1991; Roediger & Butler, 2010; Rohrer et al., 2010). So does the 10- or 15-minute in-class activity sometimes called a *mind dump*, during which students write down all they can remember about the readings, videos, or podcasts that were assigned for that day. The incentive for doing a good job is that you will return these summaries to students during subsequent exams. But the learning payoffs accrue in the process of careful reading, watching, or listening and repeated retrieval practice, first in preparation for the writing exercise, then while actually doing it in class.

Visual Study Tools

Because I have written at length on the power of visual representations as learning facilitators (Nilson, 2007, 2010), I won't belabor too many points here. The experimental research in cognitive and educational psychology that documents this power and the ways that graphics amplify text is very convincing (e.g., see Mayer, 2005; Vekiri, 2002). Hundreds of studies on the pedagogical applications of concept and mind maps, to name just two widely used graphics, confirm this basic research, and other scholars recommend visuals to enhance students' comprehension of readings (e.g., Bean, 2011; McGuire, 2008; Svinicki, 2004). No doubt, visual tools similarly enhance students' comprehension of videos and podcasts as well.

Learning benefits accrue whether you develop the visual representations for your students or they develop them on their own. However, they may not be able to develop their own unless you first review with them at least a couple of your own examples. To start a course with visuals, you may want to design a graphic syllabus and an outcomes map—the first to show the organization of and interrelationship among your course topics, and the second to lay out the sequence and progression of the skills and abilities that students should be acquiring during the course (Nilson, 2007). A graphic syllabus may look like a flowchart, diagram, map, or even an object that serves as a metaphor for the course organization; it may contain icons, geometric shapes, or symbols that communicate aspects of the content. An outcomes map usually takes the form of a flowchart. These visuals give students the big picture of the course content and the learning process, respectively. Students see immediately that the course is not a linear list of unrelated pieces of content and learning outcomes, which is how a text syllabus inadvertently portrays it. Rather, the topics and outcomes build on each other throughout the term. Both of these graphics provide accurate, ready-made structures for students to organize their new knowledge and skills on a "grand" (course-level) scale, and students must have some kind of structure; without it, they cannot learn the material on a deep, conceptual level and cannot retain it for long (R. C. Anderson, 1984; Bransford et al., 2000; Rhem, 1995; Svinicki, 2004). The mind can easily recall the shape of the structure and use it as a cue to retrieve the verbal information. If we fail to provide such structure for our students, the chances that they will develop an accurately organized big picture on their own are slim.

Visuals that you make, such as the graphic syllabus and the outcomes map, also show students the integration of the elements in the big picture, including the relationships between concepts and topics or those among learning outcomes. The very spatial arrangement among the elements implies those that are most important and those that precede others in time or in a process, helping make the abstract more concrete. Students then can begin to think about and work with the elements, such as making inferences and new connections.

Just like your courses, assigned readings, videos, and podcasts can be graphically represented as well. Such visuals offer another mode for processing and remembering text material, one that relies on a different part of the brain and therefore reinforces the text-based learning. Text in particular is a more difficult medium to learn from than graphics, one demanding greater mental effort than watching videos or listening to podcasts. While highly skilled readers like academics do not notice it, reading text requires recognizing and translating complex patterns of black lines and curves into words, then grouping these words to make meaning. This process takes longer and involves greater effort for students, especially for those with little background in the discipline or who are reading in their nonnative language. Furthermore, many more black lines and curves are needed to communicate something in text than in a visual. Of course, text offers more detail and specificity, but to retain abstract material on a deep level, the mind has to simplify it, strip out unnecessary detail, and organize it into a quasi-visual structure anyway. To accustom your students to using graphics to organize and retain the material in the readings, you might concept- or mind-map one or two assignments early in the term. In addition to serving as models for their own reading maps, your maps can help students anticipate the structure of later readings.

Giving students visual learning tools clearly facilitates their learning and retention but doesn't necessarily enhance their self-regulated skills. To help them in this latter capacity, the visuals have to emerge from their own minds. When they map a reading, video, or podcast, they have to create and observe their own integrative structuring of the material and then draw it. This exercise not only makes them organize their new knowledge but also makes them aware of their understanding of the material at the deepest level. Since students are very likely to retain long-term what they themselves create, you need to ensure that they receive prompt feedback on the accuracy of their early sketches. You can furnish it, or you can put students in groups to provide it. As a review activity for exams, students should visually represent not only individual readings, videos, and podcasts but also collections of them, integrated with what they have learned in class (Peirce, 2006).

Your students may already be familiar with graphic representations from their previous courses, or they may catch onto them right away just by studying the few examples that you supply. But if not, teaching students how to make graphic representations themselves is easy. Let's look at concept mapping as an example because it is popular and perfect for displaying hierarchically organized knowledge. Disciplines typically organize their concepts and principles this way, from the most inclusive/general/broad/abstract (called the "superordinate") to the most exclusive/specific/narrow/concrete (called the "subordinate"). After running your students through this exercise (Wandersee, 2002b) as a group activity, they should be able to start drawing their own concept maps.

1. Pick out 12 to 15 interrelated concepts, topics, or categories (called "concepts" from now on) with which your students are already acquainted. These concepts may be from a course they should have already taken or from common knowledge. Display these concepts in random order on the board or on a slide.

2. Put your students into groups and have each group write down each concept on a sticky note or small index card.

3. Ask each group to identify the main concept—the most general, broad, and inclusive one—and to write it at the top and center of a large piece of paper. To ensure that the groups get a solid start, have a spokesperson for the group explain its choice and change it as desired.

4. Tell each group to rank-order or cluster the remaining concepts from the most general, broad, and inclusive to the most specific, narrow, and exclusive, then to arrange them in a linkable hierarchy—roughly into a pyramid.

5. Have the groups put their hierarchy on a piece of paper with enclosures around concepts and links between directly related concepts. (No arrows are needed because down is the assumed direction.) They should then label the linking lines with short descriptors of the relationship, such as "one type of," "for example," "precedes," "includes," "manifests as," or "leads to." The linked concepts along with the labeled links are called "propositions."

6. Finally, ask the groups to look for, draw in, and label "cross-links," which are relationships between concepts on different branches. Some concept-mapping proponents recommend drawing cross-links as dotted lines. In any case, they should be looped around other linking lines and not drawn across them.

Invite at least some of the groups to display and explain their hierarchy to the rest of the class. Not all the maps may be exactly alike, but they may still be accurate. However, identify and correct any definite mistakes. Before you point them out, ask the rest of the class to voice their disagreements with a group's arrangement of concepts.

This entire exercise may take a half hour, but it teaches students more than concept mapping. They receive practice in abstract, critical thinking operations such as analysis and classification.

Mind mapping is similar, except that the main idea is located in the center, and the next level of related (secondary) ideas radiate out from the center linked by lines with arrows. The tertiary ideas in turn radiate out from the secondary ones, and so on. Mind maps often but not always label the links, but they explicitly use color to distinguish major links and add icons and symbols as memory cues. (The web has many text and video sites on how to mind map.) Of course, concept maps can also add color and images.

Concept maps and mind maps are just two of many different kinds of graphics. Lesser known are concept circle diagrams, which can illustrate complex relationships among concepts, topics, categories, principles, and even mathematical equations (Nilson, 2010). The Venn diagram is the most commonly used concept circle diagram. A few guidelines apply (Wandersee, 2002a). The sizes of the circles in the diagram should reflect their relative importance, number of observations or examples, variable values, or levels of generality. The degree of overlap between two or more circles should indicate the proportion of observations or examples that the concepts share. Concepts may be totally separate, partially overlapping, or totally overlapping, or one may completely encompass one or more other concepts (Wandersee, 2002a).

Students can draw more than relationships among concepts. They can use a simple circle to illustrate a cycle or more elaborate flowcharts and diagrams to represent a sequence of events or operations or a causal process through time. Still another type of visual is the memory or knowledge matrix, which is useful when the material focuses on different types, classes, or categories of concepts, people, theories, principles, events, phenomena, equations, or things, especially when you want your students to focus on the differences among them. You might give your students an empty matrix with the important categories down the far left column and dimensions of contrast across the top row. Students can fill in the empty cells as they read or when they finish (Angelo & Cross, 1993).

Self-Regulated Reading, Watching, and Listening as Essential Activities

In most college-level courses, readings, videos, and podcasts provide the students' first exposure to new material. We usually depend on these modes to convey basic disciplinary knowledge, and students probably depend on these modes most to continue learning throughout their adulthood. Yet few students come to us as strong readers, and the quality of their viewing and listening skills may or may not be better. Therefore, turning them into self-regulated knowledge consumers—ensuring that they can accurately appraise and improve their comprehension and retention—may be as important as teaching our content.

4

SELF-REGULATED LEARNING FROM LIVE LECTURES

O
ver the past couple of decades, lectures have received a bad rap as an ineffective, student-passive teaching method. But lecturing is still popular and does have its purposes. It can even hold student attention when delivered dynamically, organized logically, and broken up intermittently by brief activities during which the students apply, analyze, or otherwise work with the new content they just received (Nilson, 2010). Perhaps the reason that lectures have fallen into disrepute is the poor quality of the self-regulation skills of so many of our students. Listening to a lecture is much like reading a chapter. Learning from either one requires keen mental focus, persistence, and reflective, inquiring interaction with the material. In addition, having a purpose—such as points to look for or questions to answer—helps listeners and readers concentrate. Let's look at some in-class activities designed to enhance students' self-regulated learning skills during a lecture.

Prelecture Activity: Active Knowledge Sharing

Active knowledge sharing resembles a knowledge survey but occurs at the beginning of a class session. You provide students with a list of questions related to the subject matter of the day's class. These questions may present concepts to define, people or relationships to identify, statements to assess as valid or not, causes or effects of phenomena to explain, or data to interpret. Students then pair up to answer the questions as best they can, after which they converse with another pair to try to answer the questions that stumped them. Finally, you call on samples of pairs or pair groupings to explain their answers. This exercise activates students' prior knowledge, tells you where to start on the topic, and reveals your students' misconceptions so that you can address them explicitly (Cuseo, 2002). As a means to enhance self-regulated learning, active knowledge sharing makes students aware of what they know and don't know about the subject matter and cues them on what to listen for in class.

During-the-Lecture Activities

Some of these activities are classic student-active lecture breaks that are designed to restore students' ability to focus on the lecture or to reinforce their understanding of the material on a conceptual or applied level. The following activities also build self-regulated learning skills.

Clicker Questions (ConcepTests)

Clicker questions, also known as ConcepTests, represent a technique developed by Mazur (1997) years before personal response systems (clickers) found their way into the classroom. At the end of a 15- to 25-minute minilecture, you display on a slide a multiple-choice item—preferably one that tests students' conceptual understanding of your minilecture content—with four or five response options. Then you survey your students' selections; you may also want to survey their level of confidence in their choice, as Mazur did. Electronic technology is not necessary. According to Lasry (2008), using clickers or different color cards for each response option makes no difference in the learning gains. Next, you give students a minute to discuss their selections, then you resurvey their answers and their confidence level. At this point, you can share with your class the distribution of the responses as well as the correct answer. Not only do students have the chance to review the material with their peers, but they also find out quickly how well they understand the topic from the interaction. You also learn about their understanding and any misconceptions that may be getting in their way. Samford University psychology professor Stephen Chew uses clicker questions to develop his students' metacognitive skills (quoted in Lang, 2012). The whole procedure takes about three minutes, possibly one or two more to answer questions.

As a technology, clickers have encountered some competition from mobile devices and LectureTools software, which works in classes with laptops. Samson (2008), cocreator of the software, uses it to pose multiple-choice questions and to survey his students every several minutes on how well they understand what he is explaining in the lecture. The software displays these data in a graph that only he can see. LectureTools also allows students to send him questions confidentially at any time, so that he knows what points to review and clarify during the next class. Samson says his students heartily approve of this software. You can download LectureTools for free and start using it the way he does with his class. However, your students must pay a modest per-term or per-year fee.

Student Questions Identified by Level

In addition to allowing students to raise questions confidentially during class, LectureTools permits the standard practice of pre- and post-metacognitive questions to complement class discussions (Samson et al., 2008). For instance, students can identify the level of the questions they are submitting according to Bloom's taxonomy. After you answer the questions during a lecture break, students can reidentify the level of the questions and discuss the rationales behind their classifications. According to Samson et al. (2008), this exercise makes students aware of their levels of questioning and learning.

Pair and Small-Group Activities

All five of the following exercises make students review and mentally process your lecture material. As lecture breaks, they also help students regain their ability to focus in class. As self-regulation activities, the first and fourth activities offer occasions for students to evaluate their lecture notes and possibly improve them, while the second and third activities provide opportunities for self-testing and retrieval practice. Testing oneself on recall also provides feedback about one's focus during class. To hold students accountable for doing these activities, you should call on a few pairs or small groups to report on their work. The final exercise teaches students how to evaluate their own work, as well as the work of others, using your criteria. It helps them better understand your grading standards and how you apply them on actual models. Regard the following activities as examples that you can adapt, modify, or draw on to inspire your own innovations.

Cooperative note-taking pairs. You pause your minilecture for students to pair up and share the notes they have been taking. Ideally, they should exchange valuable material. They can ask one another to clarify a difficult part of the lecture, identify what they thought were the most important points, and answer questions they may have (D. W. Johnson, Johnson, & Smith, 1991).

Scripted cooperation. You pause your minilecture for students to pair up at some key juncture. One student summarizes the lecture material without looking at her notes, while the other furnishes feedback about the accuracy and completeness of the summary (Cuseo, 2002). At this point you might give some guidance on what they should do next. Depending on the material, they might briefly discuss how the material is relevant to their lives, relates to their prior learning, or can be remembered. The next time, the students switch roles.

Periodic free recall with pair and compare, version 1. In one version of this technique, students listen to your minilecture without taking notes until you pause for them to write down all the important points that they can recall, along with questions they may have. Tell students to leave considerable space between the points they record because they will then pair up and compare their free-recall notes, filling in whatever they left out and answering one another's questions (Bonwell & Eison, 1991).

Periodic free recall with pair and compare, version 2. A second version differs from the first in that students *have* been taking lecture notes until you pause. You then tell them to close their notebooks and write down the most important one, two, or three points of your minilecture and any questions they may have. This exercise can be done individually, but students working in pairs or small groups can help each other identify the most important points more accurately and answer each other's questions.

Pair/group mock testing and grading. Before you give an exam with one or more essay questions, you help students prepare by giving them the same type of question to answer in class. Along with the practice question, you provide a grading rubric. Students work in pairs or small groups to draft or outline an answer. You randomly select a few pairs or groups to present their answer to the class. Then both you and the rest of class use your rubric to mock-grade the answers.

"Quick-thinks"

Johnston and Cooper (1997) coined the term *Quick-thinks* for several cross-disciplinary lecture-break activities that individuals, pairs, or small groups can do quickly. All the activities help students monitor their understanding while still allowing them to ask questions, correct their thinking, and learn from each other. Each assignment takes just a couple of minutes, plus a few more to survey student responses. As after the activities, you should randomly call on individuals or groups to ensure their participation.

Correct the error. You display a statement, short argument, prediction, implication, equation, or visual that contains a logical, factual, procedural, computational, or relational error, and students identify it as quickly as they can. They must also correct the error, drawing on content from your lecture or related readings.

Complete a sentence starter. You display the first part of a sentence, such as a definition, an example, a counterexample, a cause-and-effect relationship, an implication, a category, or a rationale, and students try to complete it accurately. Finishing the sentence starter should require higher-order thinking or reflection, not just rote knowledge.

Compare and contrast. You ask students to identify similarities and differences between parallel elements in your last minilecture, such as events, historical periods, models, theories, methods, artistic or literary works, problems, or solutions. These comparisons and contrasts should present students with new challenges and not repeat what they have already read or heard.

Reorder the steps. You present an incorrectly ordered process, method, procedure, plan, series of events, or set of steps, and students work to sequence the items correctly.

Reach a conclusion. You present data, facts, or events, and students draw one or more logical conclusions from them. Their inferences can be probable results or outcomes.

Paraphrase the idea. You present a definition, theory, explanation, procedure, process, or description and ask students to write their own rephrasing of it. To allow them to improve or correct their version, you can put them in pairs or small groups to get peer feedback or have a few individuals read their version aloud to the class to receive feedback from their peers and you.

Support a statement. You present a conclusion, point of view, or inference, and students gather support for it from your lecture, the readings, or other sources they can quickly access in class. Of course, you can flip this exercise around to "counter a statement."

Closing Activities

Students shouldn't leave a class without reviewing highlights of the content it covered, and letting them reconstruct the content themselves rather than summarizing the material is the best approach for them. Unfortunately, we often feel so pressed for class time that we let this segment slide—a decision that can cost our students in learning. Some review activities have double value that makes saving time for them well worth the effort. The activities not only help students consolidate and retain the content but also help them develop their self-regulated learning skills, particularly in evaluating their listening, lecture note-taking, organizational, and knowledge-integration habits and abilities.

Pair Activities

Closure note-taking pairs. Similar to scripted cooperation, this end-of-class activity tasks one student with summarizing his notes to the other, who corrects any errors and fills in any missing material. Ideally, each student should take some information from the other (Cuseo, 2002). Members of the pair switch roles each class. This exercise engages students in evaluating and refining their listening and note-taking skills.

Pair review. You display a list of topics covered during the class, and the students pair off and take turns recalling as much information as they can about each topic (Cuseo, 2002). As in scripted cooperation, they should practice free recall without looking at their notes and, when necessary, correct each other's inaccuracies and omissions. This activity gives students the chance to test their recall and listening skills and to get retrieval practice.

Multiple-choice test items. Pairs or small groups review the material covered in class, decide on several most important points, and write one or more multiple-choice items on these points for a test they will take in the future. Chapter 3 similarly suggested having students generate test questions from the assigned readings, videos, or podcasts as a self-regulated learning activity. For in-class purposes, you might want to limit the test questions to multiple-choice to ensure that students spend a predictable amount of time on the task. Otherwise, they may quickly dash off an essay question so that they can leave class early.

While teachers may not find multiple-choice items fun to compose, your students will be motivated to write the kinds of questions you request because they want you to choose their items for the test. After all, they know the answers to their own questions. But students cannot write clean, well-constructed multiple-choice items—especially ones assessing higher-order thinking—without training. As previously recommended, teach them the various levels of Bloom's (1956) or L. W. Anderson and Krathwohl's (2000) taxonomy of cognitive operations and ask for questions that require applying, analyzing, synthesizing, and evaluating the material. Furnish examples of different types of items: lower-order recall and higher-order thinking items as well as well-written and poorly constructed items. Guidelines for writing stems, correct options, and plausible distractors appear in several sources (e.g., Gronlund & Waugh, 2009; Jacobs & Chase, 1992; Nilson, 2010; Ory & Ryan, 1993; Suskie, 2004). You will have to tweak some items before putting them on a test, but you will never have to write them from scratch again. Nor will you have to field complaints against you for writing tricky or too difficult questions.

Writing Activities

Writing is usually an individual activity, but students can still share their writing in groups or with the class. A writing exercise offers the special benefit of leaving an artifact that students can take home with them and review later or that you can collect and read yourself to gain insight into your students' values, attitudes, interpretations, bottlenecks, and mental connections.

Minute papers. In addition to clicker questions, Chew (quoted in Lang, 2012) recommends an adaption of the minute paper, a popular classroom assessment technique (CAT), to build your students' metacognitive skills. If you collect and read at least some of their papers, you can gauge their metacognitive abilities and their reactions to the material. To close a class, ask your students to write about any topic that makes them reflect on the meaning or personal significance of a class experience, whether a lecture, a video, a demonstration, a guest lecture, or an activity. The following topics, for example, heighten students' awareness of their learning, its applications, their affective responses, their learning strategies, their areas of confusion, and the connections between their new and their prior knowledge (adapted from Angelo & Cross, 1993; Wirth, 2008a; Wirth, n.d.). As the previous chapter explained, students can write minute papers on assigned readings, videos, or podcasts. Students should note

- The most useful or valuable thing(s) they learned
- The most surprising or unexpected idea(s)
- What idea(s) stands out in their mind
- How they are reacting emotionally
- What helped or hindered their understanding
- The most confusing points, and why they were confusing
- What idea(s) they can and should put into practice immediately
- How they would paraphrase the key content for a high school student
- How the material connects or conflicts with their prior knowledge, beliefs, or values
- How it connects with their knowledge from other courses
- How it fits into their existing framework of knowledge (Mezeske, 2009)

RSQC2. These letters and number stand for recall, summarize, question, connect, and comment. In this end-of-class CAT, students recall meaningful points, summarize the most important points in one sentence, formulate questions, connect these points with the course objectives or outcomes (or prior material, if you prefer), and comment on the value of their learning (Angelo & Cross, 1993). Like a minute paper, this activity makes students more aware of what they did and did not process, how the new content relates to the course, and what value it has for them (McClure, 2005). In addition, students have the opportunity to assess and practice their retrieval.

Active listening checks. At the beginning of your first regular class in the term, tell your students to listen carefully to your lecture for key points because you will be asking them to write these points down and hand them in at the end of class, but not for a grade. (They should also be taking notes.) At the end of the class, ask them to record the three most important points. At the beginning of the next class, you reveal what you intended as the three most important points. Repeat this activity for a few more classes. Lovett (2008), who devised this technique, found that initially only 45% of her students correctly identified all three major points, but by the third iteration, 75% of them did. This activity effectively cultivates active learning and good note-taking skills by making students test and assess their current skills against your notes. Students usually need only a couple of rounds to figure out how to improve these skills.

Student-Created Visuals

The "Visual Study Tools" section in chapter 3 discussed the same principles, guidelines, and learning benefits that can be applied here. Lecture content can be represented in a visual, just as a reading or a course's organization can be. But before you ask students to draw their own graphics, show them a couple of examples and teach them how to create different types (see chapter 3). The extra time pays off, because when students develop their own visual representations, they cannot help but enhance their self-regulated learning skills and process the material at a deep structural level. The students must grapple with organizing the material as they understand it, and as their organization emerges, they must observe, monitor, and evaluate their own thinking as well as analyze the content. Finally, they must figure out how to express their construction in concrete form. We want our students to engage in such deep cognitive processes.

Individual/pair/group graphic. Working individually, in pairs, or in small groups at the end of class, students create a concept map, mind map, graphic organizer, diagram, or flowchart of their understanding of your lecture that day. You can also have them integrate into the graphic material from the readings, a prior lecture, or class activities. McGuire, Gosselin, Mamo, Holmes, Husman, and Rutherford (2008) call these visuals "organizational strategies," along with outlining and other verbal tools. They recommend that you let your individual students or groups choose the type of strategy they want to use to organize given material. Finally, they should evaluate how well it served its purpose.

Unless you have a small class, you won't be able to assess and give feedback on every piece of work. If you scan these graphics and their creators' explanations and evaluations of them, you can open a revealing window into your students' comprehension and organization of the material. Alternatively, you may want to draw graphics of your first two or three lectures yourself and show them to your class as models. Recall Lovett's (2008) research that found how sharing her three most important points with her students in active listening checks taught them to recognize the points she intended. Students should improve their graphic iterations of your lectures through the same strategy.

Memory or knowledge matrix. You provide the structure for this visual. You give each student or group a two-dimensional matrix with the categories of your choice down the far left column and across the top row. The material should reflect what the class covered that day. Students fill in the empty cells with the correct information, concepts, principles, names, and so on (Angelo & Cross, 1993), preferably without referring to their notes. For instance, the far-left column may list different philosophies of education, and the top row can represent relevant descriptive categories, such as "Main Founder(s)," "Assumptions About Learning," "Recommended Classroom Settings," or "Recommended Teaching Methods." Before leaving class, students should receive feedback on the accuracy of their matrix from one another and, if possible, from you. In addition to giving students the chance to self-test and practice retrieval, this exercise helps them identify and remember key comparisons and contrasts among various theories, methods, phenomena, perspectives, and the like.

Can the Lecture Be Saved?

The research has yet to be done, but a study of the effects of engaging classes in these self-regulated learning activities on students' comprehension and retention of lectures would be very interesting. Incorporating the right wrappers could redeem the well-delivered lecture as a highly respectable teaching method.

5

SELF-REGULATED
LEARNING FROM
META-ASSIGNMENTS

While many factors influence how much mental effort students put into a given assignment, the value that students perceive in the task is no doubt one of them. They will see the assignment as valuable to the extent that they believe it will help them receive a good grade in the course, obtain a job, achieve success in a career, or learn about something important to them. In these cases, students will work hard to develop a good product. They will not do so, however, if they dismiss it as a meaningless chore or busywork that is not worth their time.

Having students do meta-assignments that foster their self-regulated learning skills can enhance the value of regular assignments. Meta-assignments can be designed to help students see the learning value of regular assignments and to increase their cognitive, affective, and behavioral impact. Often these wrappers give students insight into their own thinking and feelings, allowing them to realize things they would not have otherwise. In addition, meta-assignments can help students learn the course material better and consequently achieve a higher grade. Students may not initially believe this, but they are likely to come around when they experience the benefits. Perkins (2008), for example, peppers his geology courses with metacognitive assignments all semester long and receives no student complaints about the extra work.

The meta-assignments reviewed here have all been used and found effective. They are grouped by the type of assignment they accompany: mathematically based problems; authentic "fuzzy" problems like those posed in engaging case studies and problem-based learning problems; experiential learning formats (service-learning, fieldwork, internships, and simulations and role-plays); papers and projects; and student portfolios at the course level.

Mathematically Based Problems

Let's start with problems that require some level of mathematics to solve and have only one correct answer. These problems are typical in undergraduate mathematics, statistics, economics, finance, accounting, physics, and chemistry courses. For various reasons, many students struggle with this type of problem. They may not know how to classify and approach the problem, so they don't even attempt to solve it. They may get stuck in the middle of the problem-solving process after making a false start, or they may arrive at a wrong solution due to a strategic error, carelessness, or miscalculation. Our typical reaction is to mark a student's faulty solution as wrong, write a few words of explanation, and perhaps counsel the student to review the relevant chapter. Then we drop the matter, as does our student. This experience teaches our students how they went wrong but not how to solve that specific problem or type of problem correctly. Even worse, it implies that what we really care about is scoring them on their answers, and not their learning how to solve the problem correctly.

If we want to create self-regulated learners, we have to turn our students' errors into learning opportunities. Zimmerman et al. (2011) advocate students assessing their confidence in their ability to solve a problem before they start trying to solve it, then to reevaluate their confidence after solving it. (Lovett [2008] similarly advises having them judge "how quick and easy" a problem will be to solve before and after solving it.) Students who tend to dive into a problem with overly optimistic certainty and then either get stuck or have doubts about their answer soon discern their faulty pattern. Zimmerman and his team (2011) also recommend having students write an error analysis of every problem solution they do not complete or get wrong. In other words, they should identify the reasons that they did not obtain the correct answer. They then should successfully solve it and a similar problem. With this follow-up assignment, students learn how to solve a given type of problem before moving on to another type.

Zimmerman et al. (2011) designed these two self-reflective activities to accompany quizzes and exams in the treatment-group sections of the developmental and introductory mathematics courses that were subjects of their research at the New York City College of Technology. For this reason, the next chapter, which addresses self-regulated learning from quizzes and exams, mentions these activities again. However, they serve as excellent meta-assignments for homework problems as well.

To implement these techniques in your classes, ask your students to jot down a few words about their confidence level right after they read a problem and again after they think they have solved it or have given up on solving it. These jottings should appear between problem solutions in the homework and in problem-solving sessions in class. You can have your students write their error analyses and their solutions to problems similar to those they got wrong as homework, but you might reserve both of these activities for class time, when you and their peers can be available to provide one-on-one help and feedback. Either way, you have to be ready with similar problems to assign to students who could not solve the original ones. Afterward, students should be better prepared to solve the next set of problems as their homework.

One final activity worth mentioning is an in-class activity, rather than an assignment, that can better prepare your students to complete their assigned problems. Specifically, Think Aloud helps them get on the right problem-solving track and avoid false starts and dead-ends. It is best timed as an in-class exercise when students begin working on their homework problems in pairs. One student talks out his process of solving a problem, while the other records his strategy and guides him as needed. Then the partners switch roles for the next problem (Lochhead & Whimbey, 1987). When the students later tackle the rest of the problems on their own, they have already made the big leap from the abstract textbook lesson and your modeling of solution strategies to their own application of the principles. They even have a plan of attack for the problems.

Authentic "Fuzzy" Problems

A "fuzzy" problem is embedded in a realistic, troublesome situation and complex enough to defy a clearly correct solution. While multiple solutions exist and some may be better than others, they all exact trade-offs—maximizing some values while undermining others—and present risk and uncertainty. Experts confront and attempt to solve these kinds of problems, which require expert skills and experience to develop feasible, cost-effective alternative solutions and to project all the likely, foreseeable consequences of choosing one over the others.

High-quality cases and problem-based learning (PBL) activities present authentic fuzzy problems. They give students the opportunity to comprehend the complexity of real-world challenges and, with your guidance, to learn how experts approach and devise solutions to them. The learning outcome is not so much for students to solve the particular case or problem as it is for them to identify and follow the process that experts do. Only with this skill can they advance from novice through the apprenticeship and journeyman levels to the expert level as complex problem solvers (Demet et al., 2008). While the regular assignment may be to develop, present, and justify the best solution to the problem, the equally important meta-assignment is for students to describe the steps of the process they followed in arriving at their solution and judging it as the best. The exercise makes students aware of their reasoning in defining the problem, deciding what principles and concepts to apply to it, developing alternative approaches and solutions, extrapolating their implications, assessing their feasibility and trade-offs, and evaluating their relative worth. Students can also identify the transferable skills they are learning and bring them to bear on other comparably complex problems.

While our interest in meta-assignments is to foster self-regulated learning, they can also serve as a classroom assessment technique (CAT) called *documented problem solutions* (Angelo & Cross, 1993). With this CAT, you get inside of your students' heads and find out how they tackle a problem and understand the problem-solving process. Angelo and Cross designed it with mathematical or numerical problems in mind, as well as problems in fields that rely on structured procedures to solve problems, such as chemistry and law. But this technique is just as important for students pursuing the less structured problem-solving skills that experts use in confronting more ambiguous and uncertain challenges.

Obviously, students have to put some time into this meta-assignment, but you as the instructor also have to give some time to setting up the regular assignment as well as its wrapper. First, you have to find suitable cases and problems that you can use outright or adapt to your course. They must reflect your student learning outcomes and easily integrate with your course content. Collections of cost-free cases and PBL problems are available at these websites:

- www.udel.edu/pbl/problems—for physics, biochemistry, biology, chemistry, and criminal justice
- https://primus.nss.udel.edu/Pbl—for almost all disciplines (site registration necessary)
- http://sciencecases.lib.buffalo.edu/cs—for the sciences and engineering, plus links to cases and problems
- www.cse.emory.edu/cases—for the sciences (site registration required)
- http://www1.umn.edu/ships/modules—for the sciences
- www.caseitproject.org—for biology, especially molecular biology
- www.civeng.carleton.ca/ECL—for engineering
- www.niee.org/cases—for engineering (ethics)
- http://ethics.tamu.edu—for civil engineering (ethics)
- www.stat.ucla.edu/cases—for statistics
- http://library.med.utah.edu/envirodx—for environmental medicine

- www.cdc.gov/epicasestudies—for epidemiology and public health (some case studies for purchase)
- http://path.upmc.edu/cases—for pathology
- www.allergyadvisor.com/Educational—for allergy studies
- http://groups.physics.umn.edu/physed/Research/CRP/on-lineArchive/ html—for physics
- http://serc.carleton.edu/sp/library/pogil/examples—for the sciences

Business cases abound but are rarely free. To expand your options, you might want to google "cases" and "problem-based learning problems," plus your discipline. Of course, you can always write your own cases and problems, but first familiarize yourself with the recommended guidelines for writing them (e.g., see Nilson, 2010).

In addition, you should provide students with some scaffolding for developing the problem-solving steps. For example, experts don't jump for a solution; they first clarify what the problem is and classify it, if possible. They then identify what they know is relevant to the situation and what they need to find out to pursue feasible and cost-effective solutions. You may, of course, demonstrate and model ways of approaching and analyzing a fuzzy problem similar to the ones that students will be solving, or you can incorporate the procedures in your debriefing questions. As students gain experience in solving such problems, remove the scaffolding little by little.

Finally, you should study the meta-assignments students submit. Focus on whether your students actually devised and followed a problem-solving process, how they went about defining the problem, what information they did and did not consider relevant, how they determined the quality of outside sources (in PBL), and how they evaluated and ranked possible solutions. Long after they forget the formal content of your course, they are likely to remember and use at least some aspect of the problem-solving strategy that they described in this meta-assignment. So while you may or may not grade it (see chapter 10), you should provide students some feedback on their process.

For those unfamiliar with the case method and problem-based learning, some advice is in order. Compared to PBL problems, cases are easier for you to manage and usually more appealing to students because case solutions rely on course materials and do not require outside research. In addition, case debriefings can serve as discussion-based activities, homework writing assignments, or essay test stimuli, while solving a PBL problem always involves small-group research outside of class and normally requires two or more weeks. Cases are also extremely flexible. Discussing short ones can take as little as 10 minutes of class time, while long ones may absorb a series of classes. Cases can be the basis of an individual, group, or whole-class activity. They also make excellent writing assignments and essay test questions and can lead to experiential in-class activities such as role-plays, simulations, debates, and mock settings like a trial, symposium, public hearing, or board meeting.

Managing a PBL assignment is more challenging. It presents more pitfalls, can become chaotic, and often evokes class complaints. While students may see that they are developing important skills in problem solving, conducting research, communicating, and thinking critically, they resent having to work harder; struggle with a murky, complex problem with little instructor guidance; and meet assessment standards that are unclear to them (Edens, 2000; Lieux, 1996). Therefore, unless you have experience or training in running PBL classes, consult a good instructor guide on the method (e.g., Amador, Miles, & Peters, 2006; Savin Baden & Major, 2004) before you commit to it.

Experiential Learning

Experiential learning offers rich opportunities for self-regulation. This section explicitly considers service-learning, fieldwork, internships, and simulations and role-plays.

Service-Learning

Service-learning, developed in the mid-1990s, pioneered conscious, systematic reflective writing as an integral part of its method. To ensure that learning results from service, you need to give students ample opportunity to write about their experiences and to discuss them with one another. In addition, you should direct students to draw connections between their service and the course content, including the learning objectives of the service experience and the course as a whole (Astin, Vogelgesang, Ikeda, & Yee, 2000). Of course, the project must complement the course material and give your students the chance to live what they are learning. Because many projects have personal impacts on students, you might pose additional questions that probe the personal significance of the experience—prompts about changes in values and attitudes, beliefs about the world, perceptions of the people served, interest in the subject matter, self-concept, self-efficacy, career aspirations, sense of civic responsibility, and the intent to do more service.

The frequency of reflective writing is up to you. Most commonly, instructors have students keep a journal and add an entry after each service episode. Others have their students write on a regular schedule (Tai-Seale, 2001). Still others require a before-the-service reflection, where students record their expectations and concerns, and an after-the-service reflection, where students correct their misconceptions and consider what they learned. Two reflections, however, make sense only if the service experience is concentrated or brief.

Research service-learning carefully before incorporating it into your courses. Talk to colleagues of yours who have taught with it for at least a few years, and read books on it that are not trying to promote it, as most of them do. While not new, Eyler and Giles's (1999) *Where's the Learning in Service-Learning?* is research-based and fairly balanced. While the method, if implemented well, can provide powerful learning experiences, it will likely demand a great deal of your time and your students' out-of-class time. For instance, you have to identify an appropriate client organization, establish a trusting relationship with its staff, determine its needs and the extent to which your students can realistically help, work out the tasks and feedback your students will get, and possibly arrange for student transportation and insurance. Clients are sometimes disappointed because students cannot accomplish very much in one semester and leave work undone, so be careful not to overestimate what your students can do. In addition, the method can present conflicts over power inequities as well as political and social values.

Fieldwork

Drawing on their own teaching experience, T. Brown and Rose (2008) suggest a simple framework for students to use to analyze their field experiences and integrate them with the course content. The researchers found that it also helps students gain confidence in their scientific thinking skills. To implement this self-regulatory strategy, first ensure that all your students have a field notebook, and instruct them to record in it their field observations, data collections and analyses, notes on your lectures, and notes on the class discussions. Then acquaint them with Bloom's taxonomy of cognitive operations and give them some practice in classifying questions and other assignments as knowledge, comprehension, application, analysis, synthesis, evaluation, or a combination of these. Within a day after entering new notes, have them go back over these notes and label sections by cognitive operation. As their prior course learning largely determines the cognitive level of their subsequent learning, this exercise makes them merge their observations and data analyses with their learning from the readings and the classroom as well as review the material on a timely basis. In addition, fieldwork makes them aware of the levels of thinking they are practicing at different stages in the learning process.

Internships

In this meta-assignment developed by Suskie (2004), students monitor their practice of specific self-regulated learning behaviors while interning and wrap up the experience with a substantial paper (perhaps 1,500 words) identifying when and where during the internship they engaged in these behaviors. Such behaviors may include setting one's own goals for a task, periodically monitoring one's progress toward these goals, requesting and applying feedback from others, assessing one's strengths and weaknesses in performing various tasks, and evaluating the quality of one's work and performance. You can also add reflective questions probing how much value students assigned to the experience, how challenging they found certain tasks and situations, how they might have increased the learning value of the internship, what they would tell a friend about it, and what advice they would give to someone starting an internship (adapted from Suskie, 2004).

Simulations and Role-Plays

The debriefing session that typically follows a simulation or role-play is comparable to the reflective writing that ensures learning resulting from service-learning. Both exercises engage students in looking back on their experiences, specifically their goals, decisions, actions, consequences of their actions, affective responses, and the changes they underwent along the way. While service-learning affords a real experience and simulations and role-plays only virtual ones, the latter can be just as intense and instructive because they compress authentic dynamics into thinner slices of time.

Before starting a simulation or role-play, you should explain its learning objectives to your students: how it fits into the course material, how it complements one or more of your student learning outcomes, and how you will assess students on their performance, if at all. You should also give students your debriefing questions in advance so that they will know how they should monitor and evaluate their performance and their learning as they go through the experience. Examples of debriefing questions that encourage self-regulated learning and help students make the most of the experience are as follows:

- In view of your role, how did you define your goals?
- What was your initial strategy for achieving your goals?
- At what points did you see your strategy working well?
- At what points did you see your strategy falling short?
- When, if ever, did you modify or change your goals or strategies to reach them? Why and how did you modify or change them?

- What were your key decisions and actions in working toward your goals? Which of them, if any, did not work out as you expected?
- How did you respond to the actions of other characters/players?
- How did your feelings toward yourself and other characters/players change during the experience?
- What principles or concepts that you learned in this or another course did you see illustrated during the experience?
- How would you evaluate your performance overall? How successfully did you achieve your goals (initial or modified)? How effective was your strategy (initial or modified)?

As with service-learning, a substantial simulation or role-play—one that takes over half a class period—deserves to be debriefed by students socially in a class discussion and individually in reflective papers; the previous questions can serve either purpose. If the activity unfolds over several sessions, debriefings can and should take place between sessions as well as at the end.

Papers and Projects

Quite a few scholars have contributed prompts for meta-assignments related to papers and projects. All such questions help ensure that students observe and evaluate the processes they engage in and the skills they develop along the way. While some of them complement almost any paper or project, most are tailored to types of assignments or learning outcomes.

For example, to accompany a research paper or project, you may want your students to write about their research process: where they looked for sources, how they selected them for inclusion, what they learned about sources, who helped them during the process, and what they found frustrating (Mezeske, 2009). You might also ask them what findings surprised them or stood out in their minds. Such a meta-assignment reduces the likelihood of students purchasing a paper or using someone else's.

You may be interested in focusing students on how they solve problems while doing the assignment, in which case you may want them to reflect on issues such as the steps they took to complete the assignment, the problems they encountered, how they overcame these problems, what strategies worked well and didn't, and what specific feedback they would like (Costa & Kallick, 2000; Mānoa Writing Program, n.d.).

Another self-regulated learning purpose you may have for your students is calling their attention to the skills they acquire or improve while doing the assignment. Beyond having them identify the skills, you can ask them to reflect on future occasions when they may need such studies again, skills they wished they had had while working on the assignment, the process they used to complete the assignment, and the modifications to the process they will make next time (Jenson, 2011).

Alternatively, you may want your students to refine a key self-regulated learning skill, such as the ability to assess their own work. In this case, you can have them critically evaluate their performance or product (Nicol & Macfarlane-Dick, 2006). Using the rubric you have provided, what grade would they give their work and why? What are the strengths and weaknesses of the work? What goals did they have for the assignment, and how well did they reach them? What kind of feedback do they expect from you? What would they do differently in a similar future assignment?

You can shift the target of your students' self-assessment from their work to themselves by directing their reflection to topics such as the following: how the assignment benefited them, what they learned about themselves while doing it, how they grew or progressed as a result of it, what risks they took, what they consider their most important achievement in completing the assignment, and what parts of the process they found most enjoyable or challenging (Costa & Kallick, 2000; Rhode Island Diploma System, 2005; Suskie, 2004). If you are teaching college students who have declared their majors, you might pose additional questions about their professional or academic development in the field—for example, what they believe being a good scientist (or historian, writer, engineer, etc.) requires and what they are doing to become one, what more they would like to learn about this subject, what related areas of knowledge or skills they would like to master (Rhode Island Diploma System, 2005; Suskie, 2004), and how what they learned in this assignment connects with their prior knowledge or other courses they have taken in the discipline (Mezeske, 2009).

Yet another set of self-regulated learning prompts apply if you are requiring students to revise their work. Before they start revising, have them write out their goals and strategies for their revision (Mānoa Writing Program, n.d.). How will they change their strategies for writing this next draft from the ones they used for the previous draft? What is one new strategy they will try? How will they assess its success? What changes in the paper do they plan to make in response to your feedback (and their peers', if applicable)? How will they know that their changes are an appropriate response to this feedback?

Whether you are having your students revise and resubmit their work, and whatever learning purpose the assignment serves, consider asking them to write a paraphrase of your feedback as they understand it. Too often they pay little attention to our feedback or don't comprehend it, in which case they disregard it (Duncan, 2007; Hattie & Timperley, 2007). In addition, students with the weakest self-regulation skills are those least likely to use feedback to improve their performance (Hattie & Timperley, 2007)—some admit that they just don't how to do it (Duncan, 2007; Stern & Solomon, 2006)—while those with the strongest skills are the most likely to use it and enjoy academic success as a result (Nicol & Macfarlane-Dick, 2006). We may not appreciate the amount of effort some students must take to read and interpret all of our feedback. The task is especially daunting emotionally for those low in self-regulation because they tend to take our criticism negatively, perhaps even as ill-intended (Hattie & Timperley, 2007). Unfortunately, students rarely ask us to clarify what they don't understand, so our feedback winds up wasted.

A meta-assignment that asks students to explain what they think our feedback means is likely to overcome these barriers and reap multiple benefits. First, students are more likely to put effort into reading and making sense of our comments. Second, they are more likely to ask us to clarify what they cannot decode alone. Third, the students most needing feedback and most resistant to it will get at least some of our feedback, hopefully enough to help them germinate self-regulated learning skills. Finally, we learn how our students are interpreting our feedback and have the chance to clarify what they misunderstood. We may even decide to modify the words, abbreviations, symbols, and tone that we use in our comments. Once students have an accurate handle on our feedback, we can pose the logical follow-up questions on the effects of this feedback: what they learned from it and what they will do differently in their revision, the next similar assignment, or all their work from now on.

A final type of prompt, one that motivates almost all students to respond thoughtfully, is a letter to the next class about the paper or project: how to prepare for tackling the assignment, what strategies to take, what missteps to avoid, and what value the assignment has (adapted from MacDonald, n.d.). During such an exercise, students take stock of their planning and work strategies, the skills they developed, and the learning outcomes they achieved by doing the assignment. By all means, pass this advice onto the next class. Students pay attention to one another's lessons learned and are likely to produce better work with less of a struggle.

Student Portfolios

A student portfolio is a collection of a student's work with her reflective commentary. It may be on paper or in electronic format (an *ePortfolio*), and this distinction does not matter for purposes here. Often used for program assessment, we examine its use in a course that you control. You can choose from among three types of portfolio. The first two types described focus more on the learning process and the third one, on the learning outcomes.

As the instructor, you determine the intent of the portfolio and the criteria that students should use in assembling it. A portfolio can include all the work a student has completed in a course if its intent is to demonstrate improvement, progress, and growth. Alternatively, a portfolio may chronicle the history of one or more major works—from the notes, concept maps, and outlines; through the early drafts and the peer and instructor feedback they receive; to the final revision of the work. Or a portfolio may contain some works—specifically, the best works—selected from a larger archive if its intent is to provide evidence of a student's mastery of certain skills and abilities at some specified level (Suskie, 2004; Zubizaretta, 2004, 2009). All three variants deepen students' approach to learning (Jenson, 2011).

The student's reflective commentary complements the portfolio's intent. If showcasing improvement is the purpose, the student should write a comparative analysis of a succession of works requiring the same skills, such as critical thinking, written communication, quantitative reasoning, problem solving, or ethical judgment. Citing specific passages or parts of the various pieces of work, the student should explicate convincing illustrations that later work shows higher competency than earlier work. The student should conclude with an evaluative analysis of the portfolio as a whole to help him integrate all that he has learned from various course assignments (Zubizaretta, 2009). Assembling this type of portfolio gives students practice in a number of self-regulated learning skills. With repetitive attempts to improve performance, students gain a deeper and more concrete understanding of the target skills, including what they look like in a piece of work. In addition, they learn to set goals for each successive piece of work and to assess that work against their goals and previous work. Through this continual self-assessment process, they see their work-by-work progress, the return on their effort, and the control they have over their learning. They also sharpen awareness of all the content and skills they have learned in the course.

If the portfolio tracks the evolution of one or more substantial pieces of work, a student's commentary should explain how her goals progressed through the stages and how each stage elaborated, modified, and refined the earlier version(s) of the work. In the process of preparing multiple drafts in response to feedback, students accrue many of the same self-regulated learning benefits as from the previous kind of portfolio: a deeper, more concrete understanding of the target skills, practice in goal-setting and self-assessment across the revisions, a clear view of their learning and improvement, and a sense of responsibility for their own progress. But since this type of portfolio encompasses the earliest developmental stages of a work, students also experience what the full production process of a high-quality piece of work involves, learning how to lay the foundation for and construct excellence from the ground up. Of course, to reap this rich learning harvest, an instructor must require students to advance through every step and hold their final product to the highest reasonable standards.

Finally, if the portfolio's objective is documenting achievement, the student should select one or more artifacts that demonstrate the desired level of the target skills and abilities and explain how each of them meets the criteria. To complete the task, students must develop competence in some self-regulation skills that other types of portfolios do not require. For instance, they must understand not only the target skills and abilities but also the standard that their artifacts must attain. Only from there can they evaluate the various pieces of work in their archive and decide which items to include as evidence of achieving specific outcomes. Their justifications constitute an integral part of the portfolio.

Of course, you can add personal prompts to any of these portfolios to increase self-regulated learning value, such as: what students learned about their own character or learning process while doing the portfolio; which parts of the process they found most rewarding; which parts they found easiest or most challenging; which item, in their opinion, represents their best work; which item they most enjoyed producing; which item they found most challenging to produce; and which item they considered most valuable for their future (adapted from Rhode Island Diploma System, 2005; Suskie, 2004). If you have explicitly familiarized your students with self-regulated learning strategies, you might also ask them which ones they used and developed most fully, which ones they had never practiced before, which ones they had the most difficulty doing, and which ones they found the most valuable.

Let's extend this last idea into yet another kind of portfolio, one consisting of all the self-regulated learning assignments that students have completed in a course. Call it a "self-regulated learning portfolio," and it can be the endpoint in the process of integrating self-regulated learning in your course design. Geology professor Dexter Perkins (2008) assigns a series of reflective metacognitive essays in all his courses and has his students assemble them into a portfolio. In some of his classes, he collects the portfolios every two weeks to encourage students to keep up with their essays and to reinforce the key role the portfolio plays in his courses. A logical capstone component is a final "reflection on the reflections," in which students analyze their progress in becoming self-regulated learners—an excellent idea. Perkins used to require it, but he recently decided not to because he demands so much other reflective writing of his students (personal correspondence, December 8, 2012). You can read about how he weaves self-regulated learning elements through his courses in chapter 12.

Value Adding to Education

The meta-assignments reviewed in this chapter add learning value to regular assignments in a number of ways. First, they heighten students' awareness of the course content and skills that the regular assignments are helping them learn. Rather than dismissing the work as another box to check on their way to the end of the course, students gain motivation to produce quality work and consequently learn more substantively than they otherwise would. Second, meta-assignments develop students' self-regulated learning skills, which enable them to learn the material better and at a deeper level (see chapter 1). Third, self-regulated learning skills are well worth acquiring in themselves. They help students learn not only content and other skills but also how to learn, which includes goal setting, strategizing, self-observation, self-testing, reflection, and self-evaluation. Remember, too, the intellectual character traits that accompany learning how to learn on the deepest level: self-discipline, motivation, perseverance, responsibility, introspective honesty, open-mindedness, self-examination, and the pursuit of truth and excellence. Not that you're likely to elevate your students' character just by prompting them to reflect on how they solved a problem, improved their writing, or even changed their perspective on some facet of reality, but the more times they are prompted to pause and peer inside of their minds and hearts, the wiser and more learning-oriented they are likely to become.

6

SELF-REGULATED LEARNING
FROM EXAMS AND QUIZZES

Q uizzes and exams should be learning experiences for our students, and we can make them into powerful ones. But we can't do so if we continue to view quizzes and exams as solely summative assessments. We may have to modify the way we think about them. Without making any changes to our testing and grading systems we can look at them as both summative and formative—that is, as occasions for feedback, correction, and improvement as well as grades. Perhaps we should also see exams and quizzes as serving a larger purpose—not just to test content mastery and subject-related skills, but also to help our students gauge the effectiveness of their study and test-preparation strategies. After all, learning how to learn the material is just as important as learning the material and may prove the more enduring lesson (Fink, 2003). We don't have to assess the effectiveness of our students' strategies separately because such assessment is reflected in their subject-matter grades. Rather, our students will be assessing their strategies themselves and, if they care about their performance, improving them accordingly.

The previous chapter suggested two ways to turn typical mathematical problem-solving exercises into learning experiences: first, have students express their confidence in their ability to solve a problem before they start trying to solve it, then reevaluate their confidence after solving it; and second, have them write an error analysis of every problem they did not solve correctly and successfully solve it and a similar problem. Doing the first activity, students quickly learn to study a problem before trying to solve it; doing the second, they acquire solutions strategies (Zimmerman et al., 2011).

Because exams and some quizzes entail higher stakes and encompass more material than homework, we should help students make the most of these experiences. Without telling them what is on the exam, we should involve them in preparation activities that will help them anticipate what the exam will assess. After they review their corrected exam, they should have not only a better handle on the material but also a clear understanding of why they lost points and how they can do better on the next exam. The literature on self-regulated learning, metacognition, and assessment offers various activities and assignments that students can do before, during, and after exams. Some activities and assignments make students more aware of what they have and haven't learned while others engage them in evaluating their test preparation strategies and developing more effective ones. They all help sharpen students' focus on their learning (Ottenhoff, 2011).

Activities and Assignments to Prepare for Exams

An obvious preparation technique is to give your students a practice exam and return it graded in plenty of time for them to study their weaker areas. Fortunately less time-consuming options are available.

Student-Developed Test Questions

Having your students, whether in small groups or as individuals, make up multiple-choice and other objective items for the next quiz or exam is a classic multipurpose activity. Of course, it induces students to review the material and decide what is important. But it is also a particularly rich self-regulated learning exercise when students must also classify their questions by cognitive operation according to Bloom's (1956) or L. W. Anderson and Krathwohl's (2000) taxonomy. As we saw in earlier chapters, this activity works well as a homework assignment to complement the readings or as a closing activity for a class period.

Like faculty, students need some training in composing clear, well-constructed multiple-choice and other objective items, especially those that assess higher-order thinking. I mentioned earlier several resources that provide sound advice (e.g., Gronlund & Waugh, 2009; Jacobs & Chase, 1992; Nilson, 2010; Ory & Ryan, 1993; Suskie, 2004). As I also advised earlier, give students practice in classifying some questions you provide, according to either Bloom's (1956) or L. W. Anderson and Krathwohl's (2000) taxonomy. Once they are familiar with the taxonomy, ask them to write items requiring any kind of higher-order thinking, such as analytic or evaluative. Students may not submit excellent items at first, and you will no doubt have to edit their questions. But allow me to reiterate that they will try their darnedest to give you well-written items of whatever kind you request because they want you to choose their items for the test; they know the answers to their own questions. In addition, they don't want their peers angry at them for composing items that are too difficult or tricky.

Student-Created Review Sheet

The student-created review sheet activity is adapted from Suskie's (2004) idea of an instructor-developed review sheet that she calls a "test blueprint." If students create the blueprint, the task becomes a self-regulated learning activity, turning their attention to what they have learned in the period of time that the upcoming exam covers and encouraging them to self-test and evaluate their competency to work with the material in various ways. While the activity can be homework that individual students complete, the first three of the following four steps would constitute an engaging review session tailored to group work. You should pool groups' ideas and correct them as needed.

1. Students list the major content areas—a brainstorming activity.
2. Students designate the relative importance of each content area as the percentage of the exam that each area deserves. This step may spark lively debate.
3. Within each content area, students list what they think they should be able to do or demonstrate with that content. Counsel them to avoid internal-state verbs like "know" and "understand," and instead to use active verbs like "recognize," "identify," "reproduce," "interpret," "apply," "solve," "analyze," "compare and contrast," "draw relationships between," "argue," "evaluate," and "create."
4. Students then prepare to do or demonstrate these learning outcomes. As time allows, they may start during the review session and continue later in study groups and on their own.

Of course, you need to give the last word on the learning outcomes that students should prepare to demonstrate. Students may forget some important ones or have trouble getting their minds around any cognitive operation beyond recognizing and reproducing. The student-created review sheet is another activity for which you should teach students either Bloom's (1956) or L. W. Anderson and Krathwohl's (2000) taxonomy. You might also supply them with lists of verbs that capture different facets of each cognitive operation. Such lists appear in Nilson (2010) as well as at the following sites:

- www.teach-nology.com/worksheets/time_savers/bloom/
- www.odu.edu/educ/roverbau/Bloom/blooms_taxonomy.htm
- www.au.af.mil/au/awc/awcgate/edref/bloom.htm,
- www.olemiss.edu/cwr/workshops/bloomsverbsmatrix.doc
- www.cwsei.ubc.ca/resources/files/ClickerWorkshopMaterials/Bloom's_Taxonomy's-GREEN.pdf

Preexam Knowledge Surveys

Knowledge surveys first appeared in chapter 2 as a self-regulated learning activity for the beginning of a course, and they are best repeated at the end to show students all the new content and skills they have learned. Recall that a knowledge survey is a questionnaire that asks students to rate their confidence in their ability to answer questions and perform tasks that a course will address or has already addressed (Nuhfer, 1996; Nuhfer & Knipp, 2003; Wirth & Perkins, 2008a). Students rate their confidence on a simple ordinal scale (e.g., "Very confident," "Somewhat confident," "Not sure," and "Not at all confident") or using the more elaborate options that Wirth and Perkins developed (2005, p. 2)—for example, "I do not understand the question or task," or "I do not understand the technical terms," or "I do not think I can give a correct answer."

Yu, Wenk, and Ludwig (2008) recommend developing knowledge surveys to help students prepare for exams. The authors suggest that an instructor use for the survey items from prior exams covering the same material. The students then assess their ability to answer questions and perform tasks like those that will appear on their exam. The survey familiarizes students with the exam objectives, reveals the content and skill areas in which they are currently weak and strong, and helps them narrow the foci of their study. This activity also encourages goal setting and self-testing.

Activities During an Exam

Students not only solve problems during a quiz or exam but they also rate their confidence in their ability to solve each problem first before they tackle it and again after solving it. This activity was one of the self-reflective activities that Zimmerman et al. (2011) used in their study, which showed that it significantly reduced students' overconfidence and improved the accuracy of their self-evaluations over a semester.

In a more elaborate variation on the confidence theme, Isaacson and Was (2010) propose incorporating a kind of a knowledge survey into an exam, a strategy adaptable to any objective items. The interesting twist on their method is that the cognitive level of the item and the student's confidence in her answer affects her grade. Before the exam, the instructor designates the cognitive level of each item as level I (knowledge and comprehension), level II (application), or level III (structure of the material, analogy, and hierarchy). During the exam, the students then rate their confidence in the responses they choose as correct. The instructor weights each response according to the level of the item and the student's confidence rating, with higher-level and higher-confidence items weighted more heavily. Students receive higher scores for making more accurate metacognitive determinations as well as for giving correct answers to higher-level items. If they give a wrong answer but lack confidence in it, they lose few if any points; if they give a correct answer and are confident about it, teachers multiply the points students gain. While accurate self-assessment deserves to be rewarded, Isaacson and Was's system allows students to earn more points for accurate metacognition than for correct answers. In addition, self-regulated learning is supposed to enhance learning, but Isaacson and Was provide no information about their system's effect on student learning.

Activities and Assignments After Exams and Quizzes

The first self-regulated learning activity is designed to follow a low-stakes assessment instrument like a quiz and is a scaled-back version of some of the postexam exercises. The second activity is appropriate for quizzes or exams, and the third works best for exams.

Postquiz Reflection and Self-Assessment

After returning a graded quiz, ask your students to reflect on how they prepared for the quiz and how effective their preparation methods proved to be. Students can do this activity first individually, then in pairs or small groups so that they can learn about other strategies their peers use. You might also have representatives of each pair or group share their strategies and their effectiveness with the whole class. This activity was designed to serve as an early warning and intervention for "metacognitively underprepared" students (T. Brown et al., 2008). You can take this exercise one step further by recording all these methods along a line from least to most effective, then leading a discussion on study strategies.

Postquiz or Postexam Corrections and Reflections

These exercises come from Zimmerman et al.'s (2011) research. The exercise for mathematics quizzes and exams parallel the meta-assignments previously recommended for homework problems. The exercise for developmental writing shows how easily the activity transfers to other disciplines. They both transform mistakes into valuable learning opportunities.

When you return a graded quiz or exam containing mathematically based problems, leave class time for students to re-solve the problems they missed and to solve similar ones. In addition, ask them first to assess whether they had gone into the quiz or exam overconfident, and then how effectively they had studied for it. Had they put in enough study time? Had they worked enough practice problems? What else had they done to prepare? Then have them write out on a revision sheet the problem-solving strategy that led them astray as well as the correct one. Zimmerman et al. (2011) coupled this postquiz/exam exercise with the pre- and post-problem-solving self-confidence ratings in their treatment-group sections and reported impressive leaps in student learning. For example, the developmental mathematics students who learned and practiced these methods achieved not only significantly better course exam scores than did comparable students who did not learn these methods but also a much higher pass rate on the gateway test required for admission into credit-bearing courses (64% versus 39%). More stunning results from Zimmerman et al.'s studies (2011) appear in the last chapter, making the case for incorporating self-regulated learning activities into course design.

The idea of a revision sheet in which students identify and correct errors transfers well to disciplines beyond mathematical problem solving. The New York City College of Technology's developmental writing faculty developed their own version in a similar study. An example of one of these revision sheets is displayed in Figure 6.1, along with the corresponding quiz (Sara Crosby, personal correspondence, December 7, 2012). Note that students redo the writing task, as well as answer questions on where they went wrong in the quiz, how they prepared for it, and how they will prepare better next time. In the sections that used these sheets after their major quizzes, the students paid attention to the feedback they received from each other and their instructor and used it to improve their writing. They also learned to talk about their work with much greater specificity. Compared to students in sections that did not use revision sheets, 18% more of these students passed CUNY's writing exam at the end of the course (Glenn, 2010; Self-Regulated Learning Program, n.d.). Other dramatic results from this study are summarized in the last chapter.

Figure 6.1 Example of Developmental Writing Quiz and Revision Sheet.

Quiz #4: Summary and Paraphrase

Predicted Score: _____   Preparation Time: _____ mins.

How confident are you that you can correctly do the following task(s)?
0%   20%   40%   60%   80%   100%

(*Continued*)

Figure 6.1 (Continued)

Part I: Read the following paragraph at least three times, and then summarize the main point of the paragraph. Remember that the main idea MUST be worded as a complete sentence.
     [paragraph appears]

Part II: Read the following paragraph at least three times, and then paraphrase the highlighted sentence.
     [paragraph appears]

How confident are you that you correctly completed the previous task(s)?
0%   20%   40%   60%   80%   100%

Revision Sheet for Quiz #4: Summary and Paraphrase

Original score: _____   Revision score: _____

Now that you have your corrected quiz, follow these steps to improve your score:

1. What did you have trouble with on this quiz? (Be specific.)

2. Now you have the opportunity to improve your understanding of the material covered on this quiz. Do the following revision exercise to show your improved understanding.

Read the following paragraph at least three times, and then summarize the main point of the paragraph. Remember that the main idea MUST be worded as a complete sentence. Then paraphrase the highlighted sentence.
[paragraph appears, one not in the quiz]

Summary:

Paraphrase:

3. Think about how you prepared for the original quiz and the score you got on it.

a) Describe what you did to prepare for the original quiz.

b) Now explain what you will do to prepare for the next quiz. (For example, will you do the assigned homework? Will you study the material with a tutor/teacher/study partner?)

Source: Adapted with permission from Sara Crosby, assistant director of Academic Affairs, Kingsborough Community College, CUNY.

Immediate Postexam Self-Assessment

Add a few questions to the end of your exam that ask students about their test performance and preparation. Assure them that their responses will not affect their grade. Leave a few minutes at the end of an exam for students to answer the questions, and do not accept exams unless this final section is completed. Barkley (2009) suggests posing questions such as the following:

1. What do you think your score/grade will be on this exam?
2. On a scale from 1 to 10, about how much effort did you put into studying for this exam?
3. How many hours did you study for this exam?
4. How did you study for this exam? That is, what study techniques did you use? For instance, did you take notes on the readings? Did you write or recite summaries of them? Did you talk about the course material with other students? Did you make and use flash cards to learn the terms (or equations)? Did you test yourself in some other way?
5. Which parts of the exam did you find the most difficult? Which parts did you find the easiest? Why?

Alternatively, you can have students answer questions like those listed previously just before they take an exam (Dexter Perkins, personal correspondence, December 8, 2012) or just before you give back their graded exams (Achacoso, 2004).

When you return the graded exams, your students will see their answers to these questions again, but they will reexamine their responses in view of their actual grade and your feedback on their exam. Consider this a teachable moment. Give your students the opportunity to glean some lessons as they compare their actual performance with their expectations and their preparation efforts and strategies. You might put them into small groups to discuss the differences in scores, especially the discrepancies that surprise or baffle them, and their preparation strategies. Perhaps more successful peers can explain why spending three hours of only rereading their highlighted text in the book and the PowerPoint slides you showed in class proved insufficient and ineffective.

This immediate postexam self-assessment builds self-regulated learning skills in several ways. First, it makes students reflect on and predict their overall performance before they forget their exam answers or check them against course material. Self-assessment also makes them take stock of how they prepared for the exam, although they may not be able to evaluate the effectiveness of their methods until they receive their graded exams. However, students who were truly thrown by the exam may be able to figure out the reasons by examining how and how much they studied. Second, once students see their exam, they get a reality check; any overconfidence about their performance becomes obvious to them, perhaps painfully so. In the context of an exam, this lesson carries an emotional charge that makes it more memorable than one associated with routine homework. Third, students can take a hard look at whether their exam preparation strategies are working for them.

Post-Graded-Exam Self-Assessment

If you choose, you can formalize the reality-check part of the experience by having your students answer a series of questions in writing right after they see their graded exam. This exercise can stand alone (Lovett, 2008; Weimer, 2002) or follow an immediate postexam self-assessment (Achacoso, 2004; Barkley, 2009). Either way, students change their test preparation techniques as a result. Along with the graded exams, give students a form with open-ended questions like these:

1. How did your actual grade on this exam compare with the grade you expected? How do you explain the difference, if any?
2. How do you feel about your exam grade? Are you surprised, pleased, relieved, disappointed, or what?
3. How many hours did you study for the exam? Was this enough time to get the grade you wanted, or should you have spent more time preparing?
4. How did you spend your time preparing for the exam? (You might list activities as in question 4 on p. 68.) How effective were these study strategies?
5. Examine the items on which you lost points and look for patterns. To what extent did these items come from a specific set of class materials (readings, lectures, class activities, online resources)? To what extent did they focus on certain topics? Did you tend to misread the questions? Were you careless? Did you run out of time?
6. Set a goal to get a certain percentage correct in the next exam. What study strategies and schedule will enable you to earn that score?

To ensure that students complete the form, let them fill it out in class and advise them to keep it as a study resource for the next exam.

Weimer's (2002) post-graded-exam debriefing focuses on question 6. She has her students develop a "study game plan" for the next exam based on the results of the previous exam. Over the semester her students develop several plans and indeed improve their exam performance.

A final option is an error analysis form called a *posttest analysis* or, more colorfully, a *test autopsy* or *test postmortem*. Such analysis is particularly well suited to exams with varied types of items because it helps students identify any connection between item type and their performance. The posttest analysis requests some of the same information as the previous self-assessments, such as the predicted grade, the actual grade, the amount of time spent studying, and the strategies used. In the next section, students note the items they missed, how many points each missed item cost them, and the reasons they missed the item. Figure 6.2 gives four common reasons: carelessness (lack of concentration, rushing), unfamiliar material (what the student failed to study), misinterpreted question (misread or overcomplicated it), or did not complete (poor reading skills or time management). The table format makes it easy for students to spot patterns behind their errors—perhaps failing to focus, reading at too slow a pace, or missing words when reading under pressure. Once students can discern a pattern, they can obtain the type of help they need.

Figure 6.2 Posttest Analysis.

Directions:

1. Complete the top portion. Be specific and honest; describe exactly how you did (or didn't) study.

2. Understand the questions you missed. Write the question number in the "Question Missed" column—for example, #5.

3. Complete the chart for #5. How many points were taken off? What kind of question was it? Why do you think you got it wrong?

4. Look for patterns. Why was material unfamiliar? Did you miss reading an assignment, or working assigned problems for homework?

5. What can you learn from your successes and failures?

Course: _____ Test Date: _____
Predicted Grade: _____ Actual Grade: _____ % Total Grade: _____
Study details (days/time spent studying, special methods used, meetings with instructor, supplemental instruction [SI] or tutoring sessions attended, etc.) _____
_____
_____

Question Missed	Points Lost	Type of Question*	Careless-ness	Unfa-miliar Material	Misin-terpreted Question	Did Not Complete

* MC = Multiple-choice	ESS = Essay	FOR = Formula
MA = Matching	CAL = Calculation	DER = Derivation
T/F = True/false	WP = Word problem	

The form shown is the one that the Academic Success Center at Clemson University uses, and it is easy for students to fill out. The center developed its own version from the models in Achacoso (2004) and on Loyola University's Academic Advising and Support Services website (n.d.). Feel free to design a form the best serves your students' need.

The Biggest Beneficiaries

The various test preparation activities and assignments and postexam self-assessment exercises make quizzes and exams the learning experiences they should be. Postexam activities prompt students to examine more than their grade and to glean diagnostic and learning value from their errors. In particular, postexam activities help students identify and take responsibility for their own strategic mistakes and shortfalls preparing for and taking exams. In turn, students begin to internalize their locus of control. Moreover, these exam wrappers benefit the students who need the most help—the underprepared, lowest-achieving students (Ottenhoff, 2011), who rank lowest in self-regulated learning skills and have the most to gain by acquiring them.

7

FREQUENT OR OCCASIONAL
SELF-REGULATED
LEARNING ACTIVITIES

Activities and assignments that foster self-regulated learning can be integrated into a course without attaching them to specific readings, lectures, content assignments, or exams. You can schedule these on a daily, weekly, or occasional basis. This chapter describes a wide variety of options.

Frequent, Regularly Scheduled Assignments and Activities

The following are brief activities and assignments that you can have students do on a regular basis to enhance their self-regulated learning skills. The first one features you.

Watching You Model Thinking

Several scholars recommend that you, as the instructor, should model your own metacognitive thinking and self-regulated learning to your students (Butler & Winne, 1995; Fuhrman, King, Ludwig, & Johnston, 2008; Schraw, 1998). This involves telling your students what you are modeling, talking out your thought processes, and explaining your reasoning afterward. To add some levity, you can set up a "Stump the Chump" demonstration in class during which students present you with very difficult problems or questions—those requiring expert reasoning—and you self-talk aloud as you think your way to an answer and evaluate it (Berrett, 2012). Wilson (2008) advises that you start by asking yourself what you already know on the subject to furnish a foundation for constructing an answer. While your modeling gives students a good start, they have to practice reasoning through a question or problem on their own and get feedback. Therefore, after modeling, put your students in pairs or small groups to demonstrate their own self-regulated learning or metacognitive thinking and let them provide feedback to one another (Schraw, 1998; Schunk, 1989). You may recall from chapter 5 a version of this activity, Think Aloud, in which one student talks out his process of solving a problem, while the other records his strategy and guides him as needed. Then the partners switch roles for the next problem (Lochhead & Whimbey, 1987). This technique works just as well for any kind of reasoning that students may be doing.

Knowledge Surveys

You heard about knowledge surveys before as self-regulated learning activities for the beginning of a course or exam preparation during a course. But they can be weekly or even daily exercises in which students assess their confidence in answering questions or performing tasks first before instruction and then after it (Yu, Wenk, & Ludwig, 2008). Before instruction, these surveys encourage students to set learning goals by familiarizing them with the upcoming day's or week's learning objectives. After instruction, they give students practice in retrieving recently learned material and heighten students' awareness of what they didn't learn but should have, allowing them the chance to clear up their confusion or ask questions before the class moves on. Finally, knowledge surveys serve as a classroom assessment technique to inform you what your students are and are not grasping (Yu et al., 2008).

Online Discussions

A discussion board provides an easy means to pose metacognitive prompts either after an in-class discussion, demonstration, video, or activity or at critical points during an online class. In his Shakespeare course, English professor John Ottenhoff (2008) frequently posts reflective and evaluative questions like these after face-to-face class discussions: "What do you think you know when you know a play?" "How would you evaluate today's class discussion?" After his students contribute their interpretations and commentaries on a play, he also asks them to examine their own remarks as though they were analyzing those of a third person, with a question such as, "What is this person's approach to the text?"

No doubt you can devise good metacognitive questions to complement almost any regularly scheduled course element—for instance, "What did you learn by doing this laboratory work that you didn't learn from the textbook or lectures?" "How did your feelings about X change through the video?" "What happened during the demonstration that you did not expect, and why didn't you expect it?" "Of the several points of view expressed during the discussion, which if any of them changed your opinion on the issue, and why?" Such brief reflective tasks ensure that students think about and remember the learning value and emotional impact of the experience.

Journaling on Learning

Writing weekly entries in a learning journal helps students develop the good habit of pausing and taking stock of their learning, any affective changes they have experienced, and their self-regulated learning skills. You might consider having your students journal on the following topics (Isaacson & Was, 2010; Learning Centre, 2008; Rhode Island Diploma System, 2005):

- Their answers to clicker questions in class, including how discussing them with their peers changed their answer
- Their responses to new experiences, events, knowledge, or information
- Their thoughts, feelings, or opinions on the week's material and its value
- Their insights into how they learn
- Instances when they achieved clarity or experienced fragments of knowledge falling into place in their learning
- Connections they made among the week's readings, lectures, class activities, laboratory, field observations, and everyday life
- Improvements they noticed in their writing, public speaking, group interactions, or organizational skills
- Learning strategies they used or tried for the first time, and how effective they were
- Ways they improved their learning strategies
- How they saw the course material reflected in everyday experiences
- What they learned about themselves
- What mistakes they made and successes they enjoyed in their learning, homework, and class activities

You can ask students to respond to one prompt, several prompts, or their choice of relevant prompts every week. The point is to encourage them to monitor, analyze, assess, or integrate their learning.

Occasional Reflective Writing

The next self-regulated learning assignments are linked to content units or time junctures during the term. They all involve writing.

The first assignment asks students to summarize their knowledge and describe their interest before and after a unit or module (Wirth et al., 2008). As it was designed for nonmajors in introductory science courses, the task fosters their thinking about their learning goals, motivation, and attitudes toward the course material and primes them to find value and meaning in a scientific phenomenon or problem. The hope is that, by the end of the unit, they will see that their understanding and appreciation for science has deepened.

In the second writing assignment, students assess their command of the material at the end of the unit or module (Wilson, Wenk, & Mogk, 2008). Wilson et al. suggest phrasing the prompts in actionable terms that students can readily understand, such as:

- What material (theories, concepts, principles, procedures, processes, phenomena, or events) would you feel confident explaining to the rest of the class?
- What material would you *not* feel confident explaining?
- What material do you think you understand but cannot explain at this point?
- What can you do to prepare yourself to be able to explain this material?

The third assignment fits well into a writing or writing-intensive course, as it helps students integrate and evaluate their work. Assuming you are not having them develop a portfolio (see chapter 5), you might assign analytical reflections like these once or twice during the term (Mānoa Writing Program, n.d.):

- Review the assignments and meta-assignments you have written thus far and analyze the connections across them. How are the important ideas or concepts connected? What patterns can you identify in how you have organized and supported your main ideas? How successful have your approaches been? Did you try any new ways to organize and support your ideas? If so, how well did they work?
- Review the feedback that your peers and I have provided. What themes can you identify? What in your writing has been working well, and what things should you work on to improve it?
- Make connections across your courses. What differences can you identify in the kinds of writing considered suitable in different disciplines or for different types of assignments? What lessons about writing that you've learned in this course will you use in other courses?

- Articulate the criteria for good writing that you have learned in this course: general rules for good writing, criteria I have used to evaluate your writing, and criteria your peers have used to evaluate your writing. Evaluate yourself as a writer against all these criteria.

Finally, you can have your students write one or more midterm reflections on their progress acquiring self-regulated learning skills. Of course, this kind of assignment makes sense only if you have been promoting these skills during your course. You can ask students to assess their learning and study strategies in the course so far, how they have changed their strategies, and how they can improve them further (Isaacson & Was, 2010). An alternative is to have them home in on specific self-regulated learning skills, such as goal setting and planning, self-motivating, self-monitoring and self-testing, self-evaluation and improvement efforts, or self-discipline and self-control.

On Any Schedule

As this chapter shows, you can integrate certain self-regulated learning activities and assignments on any schedule you choose, from every day to only once or twice a term. Most of the options presented here offer an easy transition into making self-regulated learning one of your student learning outcomes.

8

FOSTERING SELF-
REGULATED BEHAVIORS

This chapter presents ambitious but easy-to-implement plans for two term-length intervention programs to improve your students' behavior. One plan gives them practice in deferring their gratification, and the other helps them learn to avoid procrastination. Both are character-grounded behaviors that involve self-discipline or self-control and that enhance learning. Deferring gratification is a form of self-regulatory behavior, and procrastination is a form of self-regulatory failure. They are interrelated in that the former facilitates overcoming the latter, but they have spawned different literatures.

Why should you bother to implement either of these plans? Research has found that the ability to defer gratification during one's younger years forecasts sustained attention in classes, high rates of school attendance and completion, good physical health; the avoidance of drug use, early pregnancy, high stress, and criminal activity (Mischel, Shoda, & Peake, 1988); and achieving high SAT scores (Goleman, 1996). Later in adulthood, this ability is strongly related to goal-setting, planning, self-esteem, ego resiliency, stress management, educational attainment, and social and cognitive competency (Mischel & Ayduk, 2002; Mischel, Shoda, & Peake, 1988; Mischel, Shoda, & Rodriguez, 1989; Shoda, Mischel, & Peake, 1990), as well as income attainment (Evans & Rosenbaum, 2008). In brief, learning how to defer gratification is key to life success.

Conversely, chronic procrastination hinders success. Freshmen are particularly prone to underestimate the amount of time an assignment will take and put off starting it. Time mismanagement and procrastination explain 30% of the variance in first-year college grades, more than the factors of SAT scores and high school grades combined (Hazard, 1997). Such poor habits are widespread. In fact, 80% to 95% of college students procrastinate, especially on their homework assignments, to one degree or another (Steel,

2007). Students may block time for studying and doing assignments, but they easily fall prey to the endless stream of distractions endemic to college life and start doing other things. According to Steel's meta-analysis, procrastination is negatively associated, at least mildly, with college grade point average and overall academic performance. Procrastination is more strongly related, also negatively, to the antecedents of high performance, such as achievement drive, conscientiousness, self-control, concentration, organization, and intention-action consonance. Likewise, procrastination results in lower financial success and well-being, more trouble-induced misery, and poorer physical health later in life.

Our students do not know how impulsivity (the opposite of deferring gratification) and procrastination impact their education and their future, and we as instructors need to tell them. Admittedly, these behaviors are easier to eradicate in young children, and recent findings on twins indicate that genetics affects one's sense of self-control and purpose and one's ability to keep learning and developing (Archintaki, Lewis, & Bates, 2012). Still, other research tells us that young adults can reduce if not eliminate impulsivity and procrastination and learn to defer gratification and to work ahead of the eleventh hour (R. J. Davidson, 2003; Schraw, 1998; Schraw & Dennison, 1994; Schunk & Zimmerman, 1998).

Given these findings and the fact that deferred gratification and procrastination have such profound and far-reaching effects on the lives of learners, weaving some intervention elements into our courses may be well worth our time. Students need the opportunity to sample the rich, longer-term benefits of putting off their gratification instead of their work.

Setting the Stage for Student Success

Whether you are treating students' short-term reward seeking or procrastination, researchers recommend that you set the stage for student achievement in your course from the first day of class by creating conditions that lower students' stress level, foster their motivation, and enhance their self-efficacy. Therefore, consciously establish a positive atmosphere of emotional safety, encouragement, trust, and support. Get to know your students and let them get to know you. Learn and use their names. Convey openness, approachability, and warmth. Be animated and enthusiastic. Smile. Display your sense of humor, your enjoyment of teaching, and your passion for your discipline. Help students get to know one another with icebreakers and in-class group activities, and build a sense of community (Catalano, Haggerty, Gainey, & Hoppe, 1979; Garrett, 2012; Resnick, Harris, & Blum, 1993).

In addition, help your students develop positive feelings about the subject matter, themselves, and their work. Foster their interest and curiosity in the course topics with novelty, engaging stories, and intriguing problems to solve. Reinforce the value, relevance, and utility of the material. Counteract students' learned helplessness by raising their sense of self-efficacy and their expectations of themselves. Buoy the belief that they can do well in the course and learn anything to which they set their mind. Encourage them to practice positive self-talk and promote the idea that they are in control of and therefore responsible for their lives. Give them positive as well as critical feedback on their work and class contributions. Because unrecognized negative feelings can exaggerate loss and heighten fear, increase their awareness of their negative feelings about their own faltering grades and make those feelings acceptable. You might say, "You may get upset or angry over your poor grade on the first test or assignment, and that's perfectly normal. Just come see me to find out how to improve" (Garrett, 2012).

Finally, make sure your course is carefully structured, well organized, and predictable (O'Grady, 2012). Set and enforce deadlines, and make good on the incentives and rewards you have promised as well as the sanctions you have guaranteed. Of course, you have to model self-regulation yourself by being prompt in returning graded work and faithful to the schedule and policies in your syllabus.

With the stage set for student achievement you can start integrating treatment procedures.

Encouraging Deferred Gratification

Unfortunately, millennial generation students have been conditioned to expect instant gratification. When working well, technology delivers on their demands within moments. The wide availability of credit and shopping opportunities has accustomed them to quickly satisfying their desires for clothing, electronics, and entertainment. While people are a bit more difficult to control than technology, students have successfully trained faculty to return graded assignments in record time by complaining on their student evaluations about delays. Students have similarly trained student services personnel. The trained have then conditioned the trainers to expect the best in fast, efficient service. However, students cannot expect everyone to jump to meet their every request and preference. Life doesn't work that way. Therefore, teaching students to defer gratification will likely save them from a lot of irritation and misery as well as enhance their chances for success socially, psychologically, educationally, and eventually, financially.

Implementing Instructor Strategies

First, share with your students the well-researched costs to favoring short-term gains versus the benefits to focusing on longer-term gains. Then consider the ways that O'Grady (2012) suggests for fostering the longer-term outlook and behavior:

Have students write down their goals for doing well in your course and for completing substantial assignments, along with a timeline for reaching those goals. During the term, have them monitor and evaluate their progress toward their goals.

Encourage students, especially freshmen, to schedule their week. They should allocate particular blocks of time to particular tasks—not only those for your course but also those for other courses, their extracurricular activities, their job, their community service, their family, and anything else going on in their lives. Then they should keep track of how much time each course-related task requires. As mentioned earlier, freshmen typically underestimate the time required for assignments. A tool for breaking down common assignments into timed components is accessible at www.lib.umn.edu/help/calculator/ (University of Minnesota, 2011), and a "First-Year Student Time Management Calculator" is available at http://utminers.utep.edu/omwilliamson/calculator1 (Williamson, 2012).

Assign students the task of observing themselves while they study and identifying their "positive distractors"—that is, environmental factors that increase their persistence to study, write, solve problems, and so on. Likely candidates include physical exercise before working, background music, regular breaks, particular physical positions, and particular places.

Provide challenging, long-term assignments that require higher-order thinking, and break them into steps with deadlines.

Set up a token economy that incentivizes deferring gratification. Let your students earn tokens for doing outstanding work or handing in assignments early, and allow them to redeem the tokens at the end of the course for meaningful rewards. For instance, for five tokens, students can drop their lowest-graded quiz; for seven tokens, they can add 10 points to their total course score; and for 10 tokens, they can skip the final exam. Or, rather than having students cash in all their tokens at the end of the course, you can let students cash them in at any time to make up for coming late to or being absent from class or to buy a brief extension on an assignment or additional points they may need to pass a quiz, exam, or assignment. Of course, students who attend class regularly, hand in assignments on time, and submit good work will not have to use their tokens. At the end of the course, you can double the value of tokens and let your students trade them in for more course points or the right to skip the final. You might reserve the bonus valuation for students who achieve a certain number of points on quizzes, exams, and assignments. Tokens can also serve to give students second chances as they learn how to defer gratification.

Have individual students or groups compete to see who can defer gratification the longest. While O'Grady (2012) doesn't elaborate on this idea, you could implement a token economy that rewards the individual or group with the most tokens at the end of the course. For instance, you might require students to cash in a token for being late to class, missing a class or a quiz, turning in an assignment late, or failing to earn a certain number of points on a quiz, exam, or assignment. Again, students who had been attending class, coming on time, submitting assignments on time, and performing well on graded assessments would not have to use their tokens. You might even give them opportunities to accumulate more for handing in work early or attaining high scores on quizzes, exams, and assignments. At the end of the course, the student or group with the most tokens would receive whatever reward you choose—perhaps a gift certificate, book, trophy, or desirable artifact associated with the course material.

Finally, *have students write an analysis of the personal benefits they have experienced as a result of deferring their gratification.* When they enumerate the rewards, they are more likely to change their attitudes and behaviors to pursue longer-term gains over short-term ones.

Helping Students Overcome Procrastination

Intervention programs work best when people are actually engaging in unproductive behavior that is starting to get them into trouble. Thus, avoid raising the topic of procrastination with your class until the term is under way and large assignments are beginning to loom (Hazard, 2011). Students are more interested and open when you tell them that you have incorporated antiprocrastination lessons and incentives into the course.

Heightening Students' Self-Awareness

Procrastination involves self-deception and often deception of others as well. The standard lies are the procrastinator's excuses for delaying work on a task, followed by the empty promise that they will work on it later (Hazard & Nadeau, 2012). These lies quell anxiety in the short term but do nothing to treat the sources of this stress: fear of failure at the task; fear of success at it because success may raise other people's expectations of one's performance; and low self-efficacy, usually grounded in deep-seated beliefs in an external locus of control that render one powerless to take responsibility for one's actions. Some procrastinators simply enjoy a euphoric eleventh-hour rush (Hazard, 2011).

Because of the self-deception, denial, and anxiety underlying procrastination, some students avoid admitting the behavior. Therefore, as you launch your intervention program, you need to raise students' self-awareness by familiarizing them with the signs of procrastination (Hazard, 2011):

- Waiting to do things until the last minute
- Not setting or not honoring personal deadlines
- Not taking action until a crisis develops
- Not setting daily schedules and goals for using one's time
- Not setting personal priorities for accomplishing tasks
- Spending substantial time unproductively doing trivial or routine tasks, reading nonessential material, and socializing face-to-face, on the phone, or on social media
- Saying yes to every request and invitation
- Overcommitting, overscheduling, and overextending oneself
- Doing a task too quickly and sloppily, which may requiring redoing it later
- Setting perfection as the standard of a task
- Leaving so little time to do a task that one cannot accommodate unexpected emergencies
- Not reading or listening to instructions on how to do the task
- Pretending to work on the task but never getting around to committing words to paper
- Not asking others to help or to pick up other tasks

Once students know these telltale signs, you can assign an introspective writing exercise in which they answer questions like (Hazard, 2011): What tasks am I currently procrastinating? What tasks can I remember procrastinating in the past? Do these tasks share any common qualities? For example, do they all require research, writing, mathematics, working alone, or something else? Are they activities that I'm not sure how to do? Are they activities that I'm afraid I'll do poorly? Or am I afraid that, if I give them the time they deserve, I'll do them so well that other people will expect more of me than I am willing to give? What activities do I gravitate to when I'm procrastinating doing a task? Gaining the self-knowledge that comes from honest answers is the first step students must take to change their unproductive behavior.

Implementing Instructor Strategies

In addition to giving students consciousness-raising lessons and writing assignments, employing the following strategies can help your students learn how to better manage their behavior and break the procrastination habit (Burns, 1989; Garrett, 2012; Hazard, 2011; Hazard & Nadeau, 2012):

- Build in some early-in-the-term in-class activities that get your students thinking about and starting substantial, longer-term assignments—for instance, concept mapping, free writing, goal setting, and schedule planning.
- To maintain students' awareness of their self-deception, have them keep a *lie log*—a written record of each lie they tell themselves to put off doing a task. Common lies include, "I'll feel like doing it tomorrow," "If I think more about it, I can make it perfect," "I just don't have the energy today," and "It's more important that I do X now [where X is doing the laundry, checking Facebook, calling a friend, reading a magazine, etc.]." Students come to recognize that making lame excuses and rationalizations for delaying action is dishonest as well as unproductive.
- Encourage your students to start each morning by settling on three tasks that have to be done that day. You can have students list these in their lie log or learning journal, then write a self-evaluation at the end of the day on how well they met their goals. An activity like this also helps them create a routine, which in itself deters procrastination and impulsiveness.
- Insert reminders in the syllabus advising students to complete certain parts of a long-term project by a certain date, or make parts of the project due by certain dates during the term. Repeat these reminders in class.
- Be sure the directions and grading rubrics for your assignments are clear and sufficiently detailed, and invite questions after students have the time to read them. Sometimes students procrastinate starting a task because they do not understand the instructions and performance expectations.
- Acquaint your students with good study and learning strategies so that they can maximize the benefits of their time-on-task. For example, it is most efficient for learners to limit a block of study time to two hours on any one subject, then to take a break. Otherwise, they tire and have trouble concentrating (Hazard, 2011). These three websites offer excellent advice: http://studygs.net/, www.ucc.vt.edu/stdysk/stdyhlp.html, and www.samford.edu/how-to-study (videos).
- Don't leave much time between the due dates for the first draft and the revision.

- Set up your grading system to reward students for handing in assignments early and penalize them for being late. A highly effective system is to let submission dates determine the amount of work required. For instance, students have to do only six problems if they hand in their solutions by the earliest date, eight problems if they hand in their solutions by a slightly later date, and 10 problems if they hand in their solutions after that later date (Leff, n.d.). You might be able to adapt this system in written assignments to the amount of writing required.
- Have students reflect on their struggle against procrastination by completing the following tasks in Burns's (1989) Five-Step Plan for Die-Hard Procrastinators. These tasks also hold students accountable for persisting in their efforts.

1. It is difficult to combat procrastination. Keep a running list of the unexpected difficulties you encounter.
2. Keep a running list of the personal costs and benefits of not procrastinating.
3. Break a major assignment that is due around the end of the term into small steps.
4. Record any negative thoughts you have about your efforts, along with your strategies for tuning them out.
5. Write down how you are rewarding yourself for defeating procrastination.

Beyond Time Management

Giving your students practice in deferring their gratification and tackling tasks early involves much more than training them to manage their time more effectively. The intervention programs in this chapter tap into their everyday living habits and values. They give students the opportunity to experience what college can be like when they get off the roller-coaster ride of stress and distraction and aim for future rewards rather than immediate gains. Many of your students will find these experiences completely new, and at least some of them are bound to embrace the habits of deferring gratification and avoiding procrastination. No doubt, those who do will change their entire lives for the better. Aren't we fortunate that our profession allows us to do so much good?

9

CLOSING A COURSE WITH SELF-REGULATED LEARNING

If you have woven through your course even a thin thread of self-regulated learning experiences, it is best to finish with a suitable capstone exercise. Students benefit richly from considering and assessing what they have learned and how they have changed during a term. Otherwise, they may leave a course feeling they have not learned much just because they did not get the opportunity or the encouragement to take stock of their learning. If you have ever received a comment from a student on an instructor evaluation form claiming not to have learned anything in your course, you are in excellent company. But you need never read such a comment again if you wrap up your course with a learning assessment exercise.

Most of the activities and assignments in this chapter are follow-ups to those you might have students do at the beginning of the course. You may recall that a couple of the closing assignments serve as commendable essay-type final exams that measure students' comprehensive learning through the course. But you don't have to start your course with an opening experience in order to have a good closing one. A few stand-alone activities and assignments are also available and are summarized near the end of this chapter.

Closing the Course Opening

As chapter 2 describes, these activities and assignments are bookend exercises and we will revisit them only briefly.

Earning an A—or Not

If you have your students write the essay, "How I Earned an A in This Course," at the start of your course, it should inspire them to aim for the A and to plan concretely on how they can attain that goal (Zander & Zander, 2000). Self-regulated learning proponents Perkins (2008) and Wirth (2008a) give this assignment to their students. For a closing activity you can hand back these essays and have students who have good reason to believe that they will get an A in your course evaluate the wisdom of the strategies they planned and describe whatever they did differently. On the other hand, students who realistically expect less than an A should evaluate themselves on how well they followed their planned strategies and when, how, and why they strayed. Of course, these latter students have a more difficult and possibly longer essay to write, and they are likely to benefit from the critical introspection.

Self-Assessment on Metacognitive Skills

If, at the beginning of your course, your students took one of the two instruments recommended in chapter 2—the 27-item Metacognitive Activities Inventory (MCAI), developed by Cooper and Sandi-Urena (2009) for science and related courses, or any of the items in the Metacognitive Awareness Inventory, designed by Schraw and Dennison (1994) for all disciplines—they should take it again at the end and have the chance to compare their answers. If you have integrated skill-building activities and assignments into your course, most of your students should be pleasantly surprised to see the new learning habits they have acquired. Such students should also be pleasantly surprised by their grades.

Self-Assessment on Course Knowledge and Skills

Chapter 2 presented these three types of substantive self-assessment.

Reflective writing. Suskie (2004) and Kraft (2008) suggest that, at the beginning of a course, students write down what they think the subject matter or the discipline is about, how it is done, and why it is important. Having them revisit these questions at the end of the course and compare their answers only makes sense. Kraft also gives her students sets of cards that Cobern and Loving (1998) developed with statements about science—some accurate and others inaccurate—from which to select their answers. They make their selections first individually and then in a small group charged with reaching consensus. At the end of the course, the same groups write a collective statement about the nature of science, how it is conducted, and how, in Kraft's case, geology illustrates the scientific method. The students also write individual reflections on how and why their conceptions of science have changed. Kraft claims that this assignment brings out genuine metacognitive thinking in her students. You may want to grade these reflective writings, but you do not have to (see chapter 10).

Content-focused writing. Chapter 2 described two final exams that are based on first-day writing assignments: Griffiths's (2010) "letter to pre-class self" and Coggeshall's (personal correspondence, 2010–11) "value-added essays." Both instructors collect but do not grade these assignments and return them to their students at the end of the course. For the final, these students critique their early work—pointing out and correcting inaccuracies, misconceptions, and faulty reasoning—and supply a more complete and correct response to each question. Griffiths puts her students in the position of a new college instructor grading a student's work, while Coggeshall focuses on how much course-related supporting evidence his students bring to their essays, as well as how effectively they explain any changes made in their thinking since the beginning of the course. Both final-exam formats make students reflect on and assess exactly what they have learned.

Knowledge survey. As chapter 2 explained, knowledge surveys are questionnaires that ask students to rate their confidence in their ability to answer questions and perform tasks based on course knowledge and skills (Nuhfer, 1996; Nuhfer & Knipp, 2003; Wirth & Perkins, 2008a). At the beginning of the course, this exercise foreshadows the material and abilities to be learned. At the end, students retake the same survey, and if you provide them with their initial results (as you should), they gain an awareness of how much they have learned in your course and how much more confident they are working with the material. This confidence should in turn increase their self-efficacy as learners and their self-regulated learning skills. In addition, students who were overconfident about their knowledge and skills to begin with should realize their errors in self-judgment. Presumably, they will be less likely to overestimate their knowledge and abilities in the future.

Stand-Alone Closing Activities and Assignments

"Future Uses" Paper

Students sometimes leave a course thinking that they learned something but not anything of practical use to them. This outcome can occur even if you strive to explain how the material will be relevant in their careers, civic participation, or personal lives. If they were paying attention, they may have doubted your credibility because they don't view you as working and living in the real world. If they consistently fail to believe you, consider inviting a few of your practitioner colleagues to be guest speakers in your course. Students are less likely to doubt their descriptions of the real-world tasks, experiences, and responsibilities of an occupation and civic activities.

You can also counter your students' misperceptions with the following self-regulated learning assignment (Svinicki, 2004). Have them write a three- to five-page "Future Uses" paper in which they identify the three most important concepts or skills they learned in your course and explain why they consider them so important—in particular, how they expect to use these concepts and skills in the future. For young students, this assignment may involve outside research about their prospective occupation, the nature of community participation, and adult life in general. You may even recommend that they interview practitioners or other contributing members of the community. Given that this paper entails more than reflection, you should provide students with a rubric and use it to grade the papers.

Skills Grid

This exercise prompts your students to recall or deduce the practical value of what they have learned in your course. First, you lay out a grid with main topics or units of the course either across the top row or down the far-left column. Pacquette (2011), a political science instructor who devised this technique for her introductory course, lists topics such as U.S. politics, budget processes in democracies, and comparative public administration. Then students fill in the empty cells with the skills that each topic requires or represents. In an applied discipline, developing this grid is particularly easy. In any case, students relate the content of the course to the skills they have learned.

Letters to the Next Cohort

These letters speak from experience in advising later students on how to succeed in a course and why they should bother. Specifically, the letters summarize what, according to outgoing students, are the most valuable study and assignment strategies and most interesting and important content and skills in a course (MacDonald, n.d.). To keep the number of submissions manageable in his larger classes, G. R. Davis (2012) solicits letters only from his A-students. Because students usually believe and listen to other students more than they believe and listen to teachers, this assignment serves several purposes, including teaching students study skills, motivating their interest in the material, and developing their self-regulated learning skills. With respect to the first and second purpose, later student cohorts of a course are the main beneficiaries. But for the last purpose, which is primarily for us, the outgoing students reap the biggest benefits, especially because they are so motivated to share their wisdom with their peers.

This assignment makes students look back and take stock of their effort in view of their performance: where they slacked off and what it cost them, where they really pushed themselves and how they benefited, how wisely they directed and monitored their studying, how diligently they planned and developed their assignments, and how effectively they budgeted their time during the term. The day that the letters are due provides an excellent occasion for students to share and discuss their insights with the whole class.

Of course, whatever your main purpose for using this assignment, you should post these letters for your next student cohort—after obtaining the authors' permission, of course. Most likely, your new students will heed at least some of the advice they read and will perform better as a result.

Bringing a Course to a Close

The last day or two of class is just as important as the first day or two in setting the tone and clarifying the course objectives. In fact, of all the parts of a course, students are more likely to remember the last lesson, whether it comes in a capstone assignment or a last-day activity. Therefore, at this time you want to direct your students' attention to the critical content and skills you want them to take away from the course. If, for you, "critical" includes whatever enhances your students' success as college and lifelong learners, then you should close your course with some form of activity that builds their self-regulated learning skills.

TO GRADE OR NOT TO
GRADE? OR TO GRADE
ANOTHER WAY?

A mong the dozens of self-regulated learning exercises we have looked at are several types of in-class activities that are not amenable to grading, such as class discussions, lecture-break exercises, and pair and small-group exchanges, since they leave no written record. But most self-regulated learning assignments and activities take time and require some kind of writing either during or outside class. What, if anything, should they be worth toward a student's final grade? They should be worth *something*, lest students think we are not serious about them. But must we evaluate and grade them, giving students so many points based on the quality of their work? If we were to grade them in a traditional way, we might have stacks of assignments waiting for our red pencil and wind up doubling our grading time. Such a prospect might discourage us from integrating self-regulated learning into our courses at all. And if we don't grade them as we do other assignments, how can we ensure that our students take them seriously enough to put good, honest effort into them?

Actually this issue is not an either-or matter. A few self-regulated learning assignments may require careful grading because they involve considerable work or assess substantial content mastery. But most need not be graded in the traditional sense. We examine in detail here an alternative assessment strategy tailored to work that demands mental effort but has no uniform right answers, like so many of the exercises in this book. But let us first identify all the activities that entail no grading at all.

Not for Grading

Table 10.1 lists 12 self-regulated learning activities that would be difficult, unnecessary, or counterproductive to grade. The first one, for instance, is a start-of-course class discussion on an assigned reading on the nature of learning and thinking. Because such a reading helps students understand themselves better, they may very well read it without a graded incentive, such as written homework or a quiz on it. However, you know your students best, and you can probably anticipate whether you need to add a reading compliance tool. Assuming the vast majority of your students do the reading, most of them should have something to contribute to a discussion. Chapter 2 suggests some evocative questions to pose to the class—evocative because they have multiple respectable answers and should help students grasp what learning involves, as well as question and hopefully discard their misconceptions about learning. You should be able to assess at least the initial impact of the reading on your students, and you can keep referring back to its lessons during the term.

Taking time for a class brainstorming session on how to get an A in the course, whether you precede it with an assigned essay on the topic, should benefit the students who need this advice the most: those who have not yet learned what getting an A involves, including the many students who have trouble making the transition from an undemanding high school curriculum to more rigorous college-level courses. Given that students believe other students more than they believe us, the weaker students will pay attention

TABLE 10.1 **Not Suitable for Grading**
Class discussion on learning/thinking readings
Class brainstorming on ways to earn an A in the course
Self-testing in recall-and-review reading procedures (e.g., RSQ3R, PQR3)
Prelecture active knowledge sharing*
Clicker questions
Student questions identified by level
Pair and group activities during lecture*
Quick-thinks lecture-break activities*
Postquiz reflection and self-assessment in pairs or groups*
Pair activities to close lecture
Think Aloud on homework problems in pairs
Reasoning practice (after instructor models) in pairs or groups*
*Hold students accountable by cold-calling on individuals, pairs, or groups, to report out.

to the solid, credible advice from the stronger ones about the importance of attending class, managing time, keeping up with the readings and the homework, preparing adequately for tests, and the like.

Unfortunately, you cannot be with your students when they do their homework, so you cannot observe whether they are practicing the best reading techniques, such as testing themselves on their comprehension and memory using a recall-and-review procedure. You could ask them to turn in their written recall notes, but you cannot know whether they were actually recalling the material or simply taking notes on it.

Active knowledge sharing is one of many pair and small-group activities that do not call for grading but do require accountability. Designed to activate prior knowledge and reveal misconceptions, this particular exercise has student pairs and pair groupings answering questions on topics that your lecture will address. During the lecture you may pair off your students to do cooperative note taking, scripted cooperation, either of two versions of periodic free recall with pair and compare, or mock testing and grading. You also have your choice of several individual, pair, or group activities known as Quick-thinks. After quizzes, you can have students share reflective self-assessments of their performance or, after you model a reasoning process, have them practice the process with each other. To ensure that students engage in these activities, you may ask or cold-call on a sample of individuals, pairs, or groups to share their answers with the class. Alternatively, after getting the first response, you can ask to hear from those with different answers. The goal is to accustom students to being held accountable for in-class activities.

Two end-of-lecture pair exercises, closure note-taking pairs and pair review, defy not only grading but also reporting out for accountability. In the former, students help each other correct and complete their notes; in the latter, they practice free recall of class material and catch one another's inaccuracies and omissions. While you could ask students to recount what their partners helped them remember, they may find it difficult to admit what they forgot or recalled correctly to the rest of the class.

Since a Think Aloud activity makes it easier to do their homework problems, students should be motivated to do the activity without additional incentives.

For Grading With a Rubric

Grading with a rubric involves selecting a limited number of appropriate criteria on which to assess a student's work and setting clear standards for different levels of performance for each criterion. Each level should correspond to a letter grade, a certain number or range of points, or a descriptor of the quality (Stevens & Levi, 2005). Developing a rubric takes considerable thought and time, but when a major assignment requires higher-level thinking, grading with a rubric is much more efficient than atomistic grading. This latter type of grading follows a key that allocates points to each component of an ideal answer and sets point penalties for deviations from that ideal. Tasks requiring higher-level thinking, however, usually have multiple respectable approaches, answers, or products (Nilson, 2010).

As Table 10.2 shows, few of the self-regulated learning assignments described in this book call for grading with a rubric exclusively, and most of these fall in the category of end-of-course self-assessments on course knowledge and skills. As chapter 2 explains, the start-of-course self-assessments incorporate the knowledge and skills that students should acquire during your course. They activate students' prior knowledge, preview the learning to come, and tell you what your students have misconceptions about and do or don't know. At the end of the course, the self-assessments serve as baselines for students to see how their knowledge has grown and their thinking has matured. The simplest option is to have students do a reflective writing on the nature of the course's subject matter and its importance. In addition, Kraft (2008) provides her students with statements about science, some accurate and others inaccurate, and has them assess these statements in small groups before writing individual reflections. Griffiths's (2010) approach focuses on course content. She gives her students a series of essay questions to answer. Similarly, Coggeshall (personal correspondence, 2010–11) administers a "perspective assessment survey" of course-content-related propositions on which students must take a stand and justify their position.

TABLE 10.2
Suitable for Grading With a Rubric

Meta-assignments on authentic fuzzy problems (describe thinking process)—may also be suitable for specs grading

Reflective meta-assignments on experiential learning: service-learning, fieldwork, internships, simulations, and role-plays—may also be suitable for specs grading

Meta-assignments on portfolios (any kind)—may also be suitable for specs grading

Self-assessment on course knowledge and skills (reflective writing on subject matter or content-focused writing, such as letter to preclass self or value-added essay final)—end of course

"Future Uses" paper

While these initial self-assessments are not meant to be graded, the end-of-course ones should be if they are content-focused. For example, a follow-up reflective writing assignment on the nature of science or the subject matter along with an analysis of how one's thinking has changed can serve as a capstone writing assignment or even a final exam. (Alternatively, it can be a low-stakes writing exercise.) Griffiths and Coggeshall view the second round of student self-assessments as their final exam. Griffiths's students take the role of a new criminology instructor, critiquing and correcting their first self-assessment, while Coggeshall's students critique and rewrite some of their original responses drawing their evidence from the course content and explaining whether and how their thinking has changed (a value-added essay final). Obviously, final exams and capstone writing assignments merit careful grading, and a rubric best assesses the higher-level thinking required in these instances.

One other self-regulated learning assignment that makes sense to grade with a rubric is the "Future Uses" paper. In Svinicki's (2004) version, students identify the three most important concepts or skills they learned in a course and explain how they expect to use these in the future. Your directions may be more oriented toward a specific industry, job, or career. While not necessarily lengthy, this assignment is in most cases a research paper that may take students to the *Dictionary of Occupational Titles* (*DOT*), organizations' job descriptions, trade journals and magazines, and actual practitioners and community members who agree to be interviewed. Giving students a grading rubric in advance helps them target their research and meet your standards.

Finally, we have considered a number of meta-assignments that offer a choice between traditional grading on a rubric and another way called *specifications grading*, addressed in the next section. These reflective meta-assignments are connected with solving authentic fuzzy problems, service-learning, fieldwork, internships, simulations, role-plays, or any kind of portfolio. A rubric is most suitable when you want to assess the work on specific qualitative criteria that have multiple levels of acceptable quality. In other words, you expect varying levels of student performance, and you are willing to reward and give credit for work below the top level. The question to ask yourself is whether your meta-assignment fits this description.

For instance, the most appropriate reflection to accompany authentic fuzzy problem solving is a descriptive analysis of how one arrived at a solution. When students observe and keep track of their complex thinking process, they should gain insight into how experts think their way through to a defensible decision in spite of uncertainties. Can you identify specific qualitative criteria on which you want to assess this descriptive analysis and define multiple levels of acceptable quality on these criteria?

You want to ask yourself the same question with respect to meta-assignments on service-learning experiences, fieldwork, internships, simulations, role-plays, or portfolios. Consider the type of reflection you want to elicit from your students. Do you regard this meta-assignment as a major work in the course? Do you have a specific organization in mind for it? Are you looking for how students tie their experiences to certain course content? Are you more interested in what they learned on a cognitive level than how they changed on an affective or personal level? Are you using this meta-assignment to assess how well your students achieved one or more cognitive learning outcomes? If you respond "yes" to most of these questions, then you probably should develop a rubric for grading the work. More commonly, however, reflective meta-assignments on experiential learning and portfolios are not graded with a rubric, no matter how long they are (Suskie, 2004; Zubizarreta, 2004, 2009).

For Specifications Grading

In specifications or specs grading, you lay out one or more requirements for an assignment and grade a student's work "pass"/full credit if it meets all the specs or "fail"/no credit if it does not. If full credit is 5 points, a student receives either 5 points or 0 points; partial credit is not available. The term *specs* is derived from software requirement specifications. A program is tested against certain specs such as whether it runs, whether it accomplishes the task it was supposed to do, and whether it meets a certain code length or operation time requirement. Either it meets all these specs or it doesn't. If it doesn't, the programmers go back to the drawing board.

Unless an assignment is quite elaborate, the specs are likely to be pretty simple: for example, must be complete, must follow all the directions, must respond to all the questions or prompts, must be of a certain length, or must show a good-faith effort. The specs define what is minimally acceptable, although the minimum may be higher than what you think of as a C-level grade. Specs grading lets you quickly assess most self-regulated learning exercises and makes them count toward the final grade. Kalman (2007), for example, is able to assess all of his students' daily free-writes on textbook chapters because he is evaluating them only on completeness; and in total they count for 20% of the course grade.

Pass/fail grading has some history in the academy, and the version that became popular in the 1960s and 1970s gave it a justifiably bad reputation for lowering standards. It was used to grade students' performance in an entire course—not an assignment—and a typical pass level was a C– or 70%. With few exceptions, studies on undergraduates found that the grading system depressed motivation and achievement because students did only enough work to pass the course (Gatta, 1973; Stallings & Smock, 1971; von Wittich, 1972). This response on the students' part was rational, of course. Some students even admitted that they learned less in a pass/fail course (Karlins, Kaplan, & Stuart, 1969). In medical schools, however, the results were more mixed. While some studies documented lower student achievement in pass/fail courses than in letter-graded courses (Lloyd, 1992), others reported comparable or higher achievement (Vosti & Jacobs, 1999). Among the other student benefits found were higher satisfaction with the program (Robins et al., 1995), lower stress levels, stronger group cohesion, and better mental health (Rohe, Barrier, & Clark, 2006). Even so, research results on medical students may not transfer well to lower educational levels. So let's cautiously conclude that, for undergraduates, pass/fail grading as previously implemented undermines students' motivation to learn and excel and therefore lowers academic standards. By extension, pass/fail grading probably does not induce students to develop and practice higher-order thinking either.

Of course, we need not set the pass level at C–. We can uphold academic standards by raising the passing bar to the equivalent of a B, B+, or even A– level of achievement, ensuring that course completion indicates solid content and skill mastery. This idea is not as radical as it may sound; it is what "mastery learning" or "learning for mastery" promised and accomplished (Bloom, 1968, 1971). Developed for and tested in K–12 contexts, this model relied on a variety of teaching methods—from direct instruction to group activities to independent learning—and on the teachers to break down lessons into small, sequenced units. Compared to traditional instruction, mastery learning proved significantly more successful in helping students learn (Kulik, Kulik, & Bangert-Drowns, 1990).

Past Examples of Specs Grading

Specs grading applies to individual assignments and previous variations of it have also proven effective in increasing student achievement. Cathy Davidson (2009), an English professor at Duke University, received considerable positive press (e.g., Jaschik, 2010) when she instituted pass/fail grading of assignments in her course, and she had her students doing the grading. She determined the standards for passing—the specs—and she was even able to set them for creative assignments. To provide second chances, she allowed her students to revise failing assignments. Her students' final grades reflected the number of their assignments that passed on the first or second submission. Davidson claimed that her students worked harder and wrote more. In Kunkel's (2002) version, called *consultant learning*, student assignments pass and get credit only if they would ordinarily receive an A. Those short of excellent receive no credit, and students must redo them until they merit an A to receive credit for the assignment. At the end of the course, students receive a final grade based on the proportion of their assignments that receive credit. Kunkel claims that his system pushes students to do their best work and teaches them the standards to which their future employers will hold them. Western Governors University (WGU), which offers online courses exclusively, instituted pass/fail grading of all high-stakes assignments across the curriculum when it was founded in 1997. This system is the cornerstone of WGU's "competency-based education." These assignments are professionally developed to assess how well students have achieved one or more learning outcomes. Students pass only if their work is B-level or above (Young, 2011). Holding students to such high standards may seem overly rigorous, but some fields should require a very high level of competency—notably medicine, nursing, and engineering—because the cost of avoidable human error is so high.

Pass/fail grading is increasingly common even in otherwise traditional courses. In response to students wanting more grading opportunities, faculty have added a variety of low-stakes homework assignments, in-class exercises, and quizzes to serve as classroom assessment techniques, attendance incentives, and reading compliance tools (Nilson, 2010). The daily free-writes that Kalman (2007) has his students do on textbook chapters serve to enhance their reading comprehension as well as their compliance. While instructors may not use the term *pass/fail*, they often give a small number of points to this kind of work if it is complete or if it shows a good-faith effort. Work that is incomplete, fails to show this effort, or isn't submitted receives zero points. This specs grading in its simplest form motivates the majority of students to complete the task, attend class, and do the readings (Kalman, 2007; Nathan, 2005).

You can look at specs grading as a system based on a two-level, one-criterion rubric, where the one criterion may incorporate multiple requirements. We normally think of rubrics as multilevel and multicriteria with descriptions of each level of performance on each criterion. In specs grading, however, the only description refers to the required quality or qualities. A work or performance is either "acceptable"/"satisfactory" because it meets or exceeds those requirements or "unacceptable"/"unsatisfactory" because it falls below them.

A version of specs grading has been used in the more typical multiple-dimensional rubrics as well. Venditti (2010) has his students assemble a public speaking portfolio of the writing assignments and oral presentations they have done during the semester. He grades each portfolio on four criteria: completeness (all required items submitted), professionalism, writing quality, and the length and punctuality of the oral presentation. But each criterion has only two levels: "satisfactory," earning 25 points, and "unsatisfactory," earning zero points. An unsatisfactory on even one criterion lowers the final grade considerably.

Grading work pass/fail on multiple rubric criteria as Venditti does is known to enhance student motivation (Rhem, 2011), and for good reason: students cannot afford to hand in shoddy work and expect to get partial credit. Specs grading provides for no partial credit; it's all or nothing. Students have to take extra care in meeting the requirements of the assignment because the stakes are really quite high, even if the assignment itself counts only a small fraction of the course grade.

Specs Grading of Self-Regulated Learning Assignments

Unless a piece of work serves as a content-focused final exam or capstone assignment, the kind of writing that students do to develop their self-regulated learning skills is ideally suited to specs grading. It is designed to help students plan their learning and assignment strategies or to monitor and evaluate their thinking processes and progress. Such assignments have no right answers that students can look up in a print or online source, and they are loosely tied to the course content at best. Still, you can set very clear standards for their general substance, length, on-time submission, and completeness. Therefore, you can specs-grade the vast majority of the assignments and activities we have addressed in this book, which are listed in Table 10.3.

TABLE 10.3
Suitable for Specs Grading
Writing answers to questions on learning/thinking readings
Writing course goals
"How I Earned an A in This Course" essay—beginning of course
Self-assessment of self-regulated learning skills (Metacognitive Activities Inventory, Metacognitive Awareness Inventory, questions about how one learns)—beginning and end of course
Self-assessment on course knowledge and skills (reflective writing, content-focused writing)—beginning of course
Knowledge surveys—beginning and end of course
Reflective writing on readings, videos, or podcasts (questions about how one learns, study cycle questions, free-written summaries, personal reactions, minute papers)
Answers to genre content and study questions on readings, videos, or podcasts (including student-developed test questions)

(Continued)

TABLE 10.3
(Continued)

Retrieval-practice quizzes and mind dumps

Visual representations of readings, videos, or podcasts (maps, diagrams, flow-charts, matrices)

Student-developed test questions on lectures

Minute paper to close lecture

RSQC2 to close lecture

Active listening checks to close lecture

Visual representations of lecture (maps, diagrams, flowcharts, matrices)

Meta-assignments on mathematically based problems (confidence assessment, error analysis)

Meta-assignments on authentic fuzzy problems (describe thinking process)—also suitable for grading with a rubric

Reflective meta-assignments on experiential learning: service-learning, fieldwork, simulations, and role-plays—also suitable for grading with a rubric

Meta-assignments on papers and projects (description of research process, problems overcome, skills acquired, self-assessment of work, development of self, revision plans, paraphrase of instructor feedback, letter to next class about assignment)

Meta-assignments on portfolios (any kind)—also suitable for grading with a rubric

Activities and assignments to prepare for exams (student-developed test questions, student-created review sheets/test blueprints, knowledge surveys on test material)

Self-confidence ratings during exams

Postquiz or postexam written corrections and reflections

Immediate postexam written self-assessment

Study game plan for the next exam

Test autopsy

Frequent knowledge surveys

Frequent online metacognition discussions

Weekly journaling on learning

Occasional reflective writing assignments

Writing assignments to encourage deferring gratification

Writing assignments to overcome procrastination

"How I Earned an A in This Course—or Not" essay—end of course

Skills grid

Letter to the next cohort

Let's take the first assignment in the table, which presumes that you have had your students read a piece about thinking or learning and prepare answers to questions about it. You can define a satisfactory product as one that provides answers of at least 30 words for each of the questions (and not some other questions) and that is submitted on time. A satisfactory product also has responses that actually *address* the topic and all the questions are answered. As long as a work meets these specs, it receives full credit—for example, five points. Anything less gets no points.

The same rules hold true for the next assignment in the table: writing course goals. Your specs might indicate the minimum number of goals your students should submit and perhaps the overall length of the document. If you wish, you can specify types of goals (learning goals, personal goals, grade goals, etc.). If you have your students write an essay, "How I Earned an A in This Course," you again may give a minimum length and tell them to be sure to include certain student responsibilities such as study strategies, class attendance, class participation, group contributions, and the like. In both cases, the assignment must also be submitted on time.

You should consider similar specs for all the reflective writing, question-answering assignments, meta-assignments, and study game plans listed: completeness, on-time submission, a minimum length, and the requirement that the work addresses the specified topic(s) or question(s). If, for instance, you have your students monitor and write about their struggle against procrastination by having them complete Burns's (1989) Five-Step Plan for Die-Hard Procrastinators, you can insist that they complete all five steps to receive credit—that is, maintain a record of the unexpected difficulties encountered, keep a list of the costs and benefits of not procrastinating, break a major assignment (perhaps one for your class) into steps, monitor any negative thoughts and ways to quell them, and record what one is doing to reward oneself. If you are having students generate test questions, you may want to require them to write a certain type of question or one that assesses a specific cognitive skill. The only spec necessary for knowledge surveys and self-assessment instruments with closed-ended items, such as the Metacognitive Awareness Inventory, is responding to all the items (i.e., completeness). Similarly, students should fill in all the appropriate cells in their test autopsy, skills grid, and other tabular exercises.

Visual representations of the reading or lecture content need a different kind of spec. You may tell students that a flowchart or diagram must show a minimal number of steps or parts of the process or cycle, or that a matrix must have at least so many rows and columns. Determining standards for a concept or mind map is a bit more complex, but one excellent scoring model suggests that you can set a minimum number of levels extending out from the central concept (typically three or four), valid relationships between concepts/topics, valid examples, and valid cross links (Novak & Gowin, 1984).

The real work in specs grading comes up-front in setting the specs. Once you set them for an assignment, you look only for those features in your students' submissions. If you notice an unmet requirement or two, pointing this out is the only feedback you *have to* provide. Consequently, specs grading is quick and efficient. You need not hesitate to give a worthwhile assignment because you won't have time to grade it. Of course, you may want to write more commentary, but it would not serve to justify your grade. The commentary would be to praise especially good work, share your thoughts on your students' thinking, and help your students improve their work. They may very well be more receptive to your feedback because they will realize that your intentions are purely instructional.

Broader Uses of Specs Grading

As we have already seen, the use of specs grading is not limited to self-regulated learning products or other kinds of minor assignments that complement or ensure compliance with a major one. C. Davidson (2009) developed specs, in effect, for a substantial creative assignment. You can easily set standards for creative work that do not dictate the medium or discourage originality—for example, length (whether written or performed), purpose, and intended audience—and your student learning outcomes may necessitate other criteria. C. Davidson (2009), Kunkel (2002), Western Governors University (Young, 2011), and Venditti (2010) applied specs grading to conventional assignments as well. Maybe you can use specs grading for all or some of your conventional assignments, too.

Perhaps you did not react favorably to the idea of specs grading when I explained it earlier using the example of a software program having to be tested against certain specs. You might not think of student work in your discipline as so cut-and-dried or reducible to specifications. However, most student assignments, such as research papers, rhetorical essays, lab reports, and the like, follow a formula or a template. As instructors, we should be able to explain this formula to our students in as much detail that we deem important for them to complete the assignment successfully. If students follow it for organization, length, references, and all the other criteria on which we assess their work, they should meet the basic standards for the assignment and receive full credit for it. Conversely, if they fail to follow the formula, they should receive no credit.

This type of grading would raise standards considerably, and students would quickly learn to follow the directions and meet the specifications. Of course, we might want to allow for revisions of unacceptable work as well. This type of grading would also raise standards for us, as we would need to clearly communicate specific directions, criteria, and expectations so that our students understand *exactly* what they have to do in an assignment. Traditional grading systems have not stressed clarity to this degree, and only with the introductions of rubrics have we furnished definite criteria and descriptions of levels of quality for assessing work.

Let's take an example of an assignment common to multiple disciplines: writing a review of the literature, presumably as the basis of a rhetorical argument, proposal, or research study. When we give such an assignment to our students, we want them to write a *good* review of the literature for their scholarly level. However, when we grade these reviews traditionally, we are perfectly willing to settle for and give partial credit to work that falls short of what we define as "good." Most likely, we assess it using a four- or five-level rubric. The top level designates the criteria of a "good" review—for example, a first paragraph that explains the problem, subsequent paragraphs that summarize a collection of work making the same point, an organization that lays out the controversies or inconsistent findings in the literature, a certain number of references, certain kinds of references (i.e., scholarly journals, books, government reports), and a given number of words. Depending on your standards, the next level of quality may or may not represent what you consider to be a good review. If it does not, then the top level of the rubric furnishes your list of specifications for the assignment. If that second level of quality is still quite acceptable to you, then examine the third level. Chances are that this latter level is not what you would hope your students would submit. Grading on a multilevel rubric, you would give partial credit for work at this third level while knowing that it was not really satisfactory, that it did not reflect achievement of the student learning outcomes it was meant to assess. If this is the case, why accept unacceptable work? Why give any credit for it? In specs grading, you give full credit only for work that fulfills the requirements for truly satisfactory work that demonstrates attainment of the related outcomes.

You can easily define what "good" means for other common student assignments as well because they also follow a formula or template: business memos, business proposals and plans, financial statements, annual reports, press releases, policy statements, résumés, engineering designs, all types of technical documents, and most types of oral presentations (sales, marketing, financial, persuasive, informative, etc.).

In traditional grading systems, we often fail to provide students with as much detail as we should in laying out what we expect them to do. In addition, since students anticipate receiving fairly generous partial credit for a carelessly done assignment, they have little incentive to pay careful attention to whatever instructions we give them. In turn, we accept and grade whatever they submit and spend hours deciding how much partial credit it is worth. We try to mark every error and omission they make and write lengthy, self-justifying explanations for each point we subtract. Little wonder that student work varies so broadly in quality. We are not motivating our students to work toward excellence. Perhaps we would if we specs-graded their work against a clear standard representing truly good, if not excellent, work.

How Much to Count Self-Regulated Learning Assignments

At the beginning of this chapter I maintained that these assignments should be worth something toward the final grade, or our students might not think we value them. But exactly how much depends on how many we assign and how much time and effort they demand. A onetime in-class exercise that requires no writing, such as completing a knowledge survey or a metacognitive skills self-assessment instrument, might take just five to 20 minutes in class. So its value should be less than 1% of the final grade, whether your students take it at the beginning or end of the course, or at both times. Of slightly higher value are the one-time, start-of-course writing assignments: answering questions on an article on learning or thinking, setting course goals, describing "How I Earned an A in This Course," or reflecting on the nature of the subject matter. These assignments require genuine thought but not necessarily a great deal of writing, so each may reasonably be worth about 1% of the grade. If you follow up on "How I Earned an A in This Course" with an end-of-course self-assessment on how students actually did or didn't earn that A, this second essay might carry the same or a slightly higher value. If you have students repeat their reflections on the nature of the subject matter as an end-of-course assignment, they should be able to write much longer and richer descriptions and correct their previous misconceptions. Therefore, you should weight these second reflections more than the first, perhaps as much as 10% of the course grade.

You might want to link exam-related written assignments—student-created review sheets, self-confidence ratings during exams, postexam reflections and corrections, immediate postexam self-assessments, study game plans, and test autopsies—to exam scores. In other words, students who turn in a completed, good-faith product can add a small percentage to their exam score. For instance, if an exam is worth a total of 50 points, they might gain between one and five points, whatever you designate. Those who perform well on the exam have much less work to do on a postexam exercise, so you might want to set a ceiling of the total number of points on the exam (50 in this example).

How much to count reading-, video-, podcast-, and lecture-related writing assignments depends on how much student time and effort they involve. Minute papers, RSQC2 exercises, active listening checks, and short reflections at the end of lectures are quick, low-effort exercises. Therefore, if we have our students write one or another of these on a regular basis, all of them together are reasonably worth 10% of the grade. A comparable reading-related assignment is what Paulson (1999) has his organic chemistry students do: They answer one fairly easy question on the day's readings in class, just to show they have done the readings, and all their responses together count 10% of their grade. Slightly more demanding are the reflective questions that Ives Araujo (quoted in Schell, 2012) assigns to his physics students about what they found confusing, difficult, and most interesting in sections of the textbook. Araujo weights all their answers 15% of their grade. Perhaps the most substantial reading wrapper we have seen is Kalman's (2007), which demands considerable time and energy of his physics students over the term. They free-write about each major section of every textbook chapter, jot down confusing points and questions, and summarize the material at the end. That he counts these assignments in total 20% of the course grade seems fair. We might also take into account the readings themselves because students might sometimes skip them if they weren't being held accountable for doing them with an assignment.

Of higher value than most reading-, video-, podcast-, and lecture-related assignments are weekly journaling on learning, online metacognitive discussions, occasional reflective writing assignments, and student-developed test questions—assuming they meet all the specs. If the standards and frequency are high, these assignments may justifiably be worth in total as much as 20% of the grade.

Still more demanding and potentially weightier are the various reflective meta-assignments linked to major learning experiences and products: authentic fuzzy problem solving, service-learning, fieldwork, simulations, role-plays, papers, projects, and portfolios. These meta-assignments require close observation and monitoring of one's cognitive and often affective processes as well as one's strategies for organizing the task and overcoming problems. They also entail diligent self-evaluation of one's process, product, skills, and growth. This challenging work stretches students to self-examine at a deeper introspective level than they probably ever have. Then they must put these complex reflections into words—easily three to five pages or more of them, depending on the prompts—and write them in a formal style that requires attention to tone, organization, and mechanics. If the regular assignment is a tangible product such as a paper, project, portfolio, or problem-based learning analysis, a reflective meta-assignment may rightfully be worth as much as half the value of the regular one in terms of the percentage of the final grade. If the regular assignment is an intangible experiential activity such as service-learning, fieldwork, a simulation, or a role-play, the accompanying meta-assignment may justifiably carry the entire value of the assignment.

The section has addressed the final grade value of almost all the self-regulated learning assignments in this book. These many examples simply suggest parameters to follow in determining the course grade value of other such assignments.

Minimalist Grading

Self-regulated learning activities and assignments need not burden you with extra grading. Only those that serve as final exams or research-based capstone papers call for traditional grading. You need not grade individual, small-group, and whole-class activities that do not produce a written product, (e.g., discussions and lecture-break exercises) at all. All the other self-regulated learning assignments can be specs-graded very quickly because all you are requiring is on-time submission, a good-faith response (addressing the question or task), minimum length (if you set one), and completeness. You do not have to accept late submissions, supply substantive feedback, or parcel out partial credit. Consider the learning, metacognitive, and productivity gains that your very modest time investment in these assignments can make for your students.

Keep in mind that you can use specs grading to assess creative and standard assignments as well. It can save you hours of grading time during the term, when your time is most precious, if you plan ahead and prepare your specifications in advance. Because you are describing only one level of acceptable work, it should take you less time and effort than developing a multilevel rubric.

II

PLANNING TO INTEGRATE
SELF-REGULATED LEARNING
INTO COURSE DESIGN

In this chapter, we consider ways to integrate self-regulated learning into the design of any course. To begin, we assume that you are doing this for the first time, but you will also learn how to build more and more self-regulated learning into your courses as you see good results and your confidence builds.

You might regard this book as a handy compendium of activities and assignments, and it is, from one perspective. It can be viewed as a catalog of techniques that various faculty have tried, tested, and found effective in teaching students how to set learning goals, assess their progress toward these goals, process and store knowledge, observe and evaluate their own thinking, learn more from assignments and exams, and discipline themselves to facilitate their success. In the beginning, you might try out a few techniques that you think will reap the richest rewards for your particular classes and monitor their effects on student performance. Maybe the next time you teach the course, you will keep the most successful ones and experiment with others.

But this book is really much more than a catalog. View it as a construction site with an array of different building materials for you to create valuable learning experiences for your students. Hear it as a call to weave self-regulated learning into course design. The many other available books on course design all recommend making the foundation student learning outcomes that are tied to mastering the content and discipline-related skills. The course then aims to provide learning experiences that prepare students to perform well on assessment instruments that measure that mastery. But what about the skills that lie behind this type of mastery—"learning to learn" that content and those skills, learning how to achieve those outcomes? Learning how to learn is an outcome in itself—really an essential one and the ultimate lifelong learning skill (Fink, 2003). Just doing decently on exams and assignments is no assurance that a student has actually learned how to master the material. She can employ plug-and-chug techniques with little conceptual rationale for what she is doing and still pass many problem-solving courses. Certainly such a student has not learned how to learn the content and skills and is therefore handicapped in any subsequent courses in the discipline.

Therefore, why not enhance courses with self-regulated learning outcomes that run parallel to the discipline-related ones? As you might expect, the most active researchers in self-regulated learning, such as Wirth, Perkins, and Zimmerman, recommend and actually do this, as the final chapter shows. Support also comes from unexpected places like developmental psychologist Dr. Monisha Pasupathi (2012) in her recorded course, *How We Learn*, produced by the Teaching Company. Self-regulated learning activities and assignments apply to just about every aspect of a course: orienting students to the material; out-of-class readings, videos, and podcasts; lectures and class activities; problem-solving, written, and other homework assignments; quizzes and exams; units, modules, and benchmarks; and course closure. Even if we bring self-regulated learning activities and assignments into our courses on a piecemeal basis, why shouldn't we articulate some learning outcomes that capture their benefits?

Unfortunately, many faculty similarly use formal student groups among their teaching strategies—assigning, for example, group projects, presentations, reports, case study analyses, and the like—but fail to include social learning outcomes in their course design and syllabi. Because of this oversight, they may forget that students are still learning crucial social skills such as leadership, negotiation, conflict resolution, and delivering and accepting constructive criticism. Therefore, they need some explicit training and feedback in these soft skills. Faculty who do not articulate such outcomes may inadvertently miss precious opportunities to coach students in improving these teaming abilities.

Objections?

The idea of adding anything to courses usually evokes two objections. The first one is the concern that the grading will be taxing. Hopefully, the recommendation in chapter 10 to use specs grading for almost all self-regulated learning assignments and to skip grading all together for activities dispelled that fear. The second reservation is usually about being able to cover the content. Will incorporating self-regulated learning goals rob precious student time and effort from the content? The answer is that it doesn't have to. Remember that most of the self-regulated learning activities and assignments we have examined are either content-focused—a few even suitable to serve as final exams—or wrapped around regular content-focused assignments and activities, such as readings, lectures, papers, projects, experiential activities, and exams. Those that take place in class are very brief and actually help students learn the content, as do student-active lecture breaks and classroom assessment techniques. Those that wrap around out-of-class assignments may take a bit more time, but they entail little stress and often teach students something about themselves, which they usually value. In addition, most wrappers reinforce the content.

The following is a list of the only assignments and activities that part ways from the course content. The first four occur at the beginning of the course, before you and your students really delve into the content. The last two are end-of-course assignments, typically after finishing the content. The six in the middle are designed for during the course, and they involve home-work, not class time.

- Discussing or writing answers to questions on learning/thinking readings
- Writing course goals
- "How I earned an A in this course" essay
- Self-assessment of self-regulated learning skills

- Study game plan for the next exam
- Frequent online metacognition discussions
- Weekly journaling on learning
- Occasional reflective writing assignments
- Writing assignments to encourage deferring gratification
- Writing assignments to overcome procrastination

- "How I Earned an A in This Course—or Not" essay
- Letter to the next cohort

Whether tied to the content or not, self-regulated learning activities and assignments make students aware of how well they are learning it and how they can learn it better while providing you with valuable classroom assessment.

As mentioned in chapter 2, Pintrich (2002) strongly advises being explicit about your intention and methods to develop your students' self-regulatory skills, which may be the most class-time-consuming task associated with self-regulated learning: explaining to students what the concept is and how the related activities and assignments will hone their learning skills and improve their performance. In his geology course, Perkins spends about 10% of his class time discussing self-regulated learning and study strategies with his students (personal correspondence, December 8, 2012), but you need not devote so much. Just one minute of class time per meeting on average should be enough to keep self-regulatory skills on your students' mental radar.

A third, less common objection that faculty may raise to emphasizing the development of self-regulated learning skills in their courses is loading too much extra homework on their students. To reiterate, these exercises tend not to be that time-consuming. But more importantly, studies tell us that our students these days are not putting much time and effort into their homework. Specifically, full-time college students spend an average of only 15 hours each week on their out-of-class coursework—about three hours per three-credit course—whether they have jobs or not (Babcock & Marks, 2011). They can do more—some of them, a lot more. Many of our students, our younger ones in particular, have grown up getting good grades while doing little homework and consequently don't expect to have to put forth much effort in college. They are accustomed to studying and learning at a shallow level. In contrast, learning at a deep level requires the time and energy to self-examine for comprehension, recall, and sources of error. Self-regulatory exercises help direct their learning to that deeper level. Perhaps you have previously added other activities and homework—writing chapter summaries, frequent quizzing, and answering study questions—that have not sufficiently enhanced your students' learning. If so, consider replacing these tasks with self-regulated learning activities and assignments and charting the results.

Getting Started

It's okay to start small. The best approach may be to lead with the course in which student performance is the most disappointing because it should obtain the best results. But before doing anything, check to see how cleanly and smoothly your course runs because integrating self-regulated learning into it can magnify any glitches.

Here are a few examples of problems in course components that can and will interfere with the best-laid plans to create self-regulated learners. If the readings, videos, or podcasts are too advanced for the students, reading wrappers serve little purpose. If lectures are poorly organized or delivered such that finding the main points would challenge even a colleague, active listening checks just won't work, and minute papers, visual representations, and RSQC2 won't work much better. If class time is not well managed, in-class activities like Think Aloud and those just mentioned may never happen. If exam questions are ambiguous, poorly constructed, or trivia-focused, exam wrappers do little to help students learn from their mistakes. Finally, if assignment directions, rubrics, or feedback are too sketchy or otherwise unclear to the students, meta-assignments cannot help them develop good planning, self-monitoring, self-evaluation, or any other metacognitive skills. In short, instructors who venture into self-regulated learning have to be hyperaware of how they teach, run classes, and assess and ensure that they are performing these tasks well.

This section suggests that you first formulate a few self-regulated learning outcomes for your students. Then, using them as guides to your decision making, select from among the following activities and assignments recommended to integrate into your course initially. These assignments are some of the easiest to implement while also some of the most powerful.

Your Outcomes and Your Syllabus

Make sure that your student learning outcomes include the appropriate self-regulated learning outcomes. Which of the following—and these are just examples—do you want your students to be able to do by the end of your revised course?

- Explain what learning involves and how this is different from what they thought previously.
- Identify and plan the behaviors that are necessary to do well in the course.
- Set goals for their learning in the course.
- Assess their progress toward these goals on a regular basis.
- Accurately summarize and retain the main points from readings, videos, podcasts, and live lectures.
- Consciously observe and evaluate their own thinking, affective responses, and actions in solving problems, conducting research, writing papers, working on projects, performing service, negotiating a simulation, role-playing, conducting fieldwork, working in an actual job, or evaluating their own products.
- Practice self-discipline and defer gratification in scheduling their time wisely and honoring that schedule.
- Set performance goals for their exams and major assignments.
- Study more effectively for exams.
- Abandon learning strategies that are not working well and try others that are likely to work better.
- Solve problems and perform tasks that they couldn't in their first assessment.
- Predict their performance on an upcoming quiz, exam, or homework problem with high accuracy, avoiding overconfidence.

- Accurately interpret instructor and peer feedback.
- Revise their work according to a plan that addresses the concerns raised by the instructor and peer reviewers.
- Explain how they received the grade that they did.
- Explain the connection between their learning strategies and effort and their performance on homework, quizzes, and exams.
- Explain the skills they have acquired or refined during the course and the contexts in which those skills will be useful.
- Describe how they have changed their values, beliefs, attitudes, behaviors, ways of thinking, standards of evidence, or understanding of phenomena as a result of taking the course.

Select or adapt just a few critical outcomes to start and let them serve as your guide in deciding which self-regulated learning activities and assignments to bring into your course. You can tell the outcome that a given activity or assignment will help students achieve just from its probes, questions, or instructions. The outcomes of having students describe their reasoning in defining a problem, deciding what principles and concepts to apply, and developing and evaluating alternative solutions, for example, are just those abilities. The purposes of self-regulated learning activities and assignments are pretty transparent.

List your self-regulated learning outcomes in your syllabus, along with your content- and skills-related outcomes. You may want to keep these separate to give yourself space to define what self-regulated learning is and explain how it impacts learning everything else. Tell your students, in the syllabus and orally, that it is learning how to learn, which involves a host of cognitive, affective, and behavioral skills we all too rarely talk about or teach, but these skills are the ones that will help them learn through life, whatever careers they decide to pursue. After all, every occupation that requires training or education changes over time and demands new information, knowledge, and skills, or it disappears and is replaced by a non-yet-imagined occupation that demands new information, knowledge, and skills. Advise your students that they must keep learning just to survive, let alone thrive. Their employer might furnish what they need to learn but definitely not how to learn it. Hopefully, you can sell them on the concept of self-regulation.

To Open the Course

Even if you are just easing into self-regulated learning, launch your course with a simple activity or assignment that helps students understand what self-regulated learning is. Having your students read Leamnson's (2002) article, *Learning (Your First Job)*, and then either write answers to questions on it (to be spec-graded) or discuss it in class, may offer the most impact. The article is only 12 pages long, easy to read, and highly practical, with skills advice on listening to a lecture, taking notes, managing time, getting interested in the material, and preparing for exams, as well as information on brain biology, different cognitive operations, and the sheer work that learning entails. This reading equips students to understand what learning actually involves and to move beyond their misconceptions.

Another simple assignment that can stand alone or be repeated to close a course is the goal-setting essay, "How I Earned an A in This Course." You can post these essays in your learning management system and ask students to read them (they probably will without a compliance tool), or you can lead a class discussion about the topic. This assignment helps students identify what they have to do to earn a good grade, take responsibility for their performance, and hopefully set their sights on doing well.

For Assigned Readings, Videos, and Podcasts

If you are like most college-level faculty, your courses anchor a great deal of content in the readings—or if you have flipped your classroom, videos or podcasts. No doubt you want your students to do this homework consistently, so you have to hold them accountable for it. Why not use a compliance tool that adds a self-regulated learning benefit for your students?

Having students write reflections on the readings, videos, or podcasts on a regular basis is a simple yet powerful self-regulated learning assignment that also ensures compliance. Among the researchers endorsing such reflections are Wirth (2008a, n.d.), Kalman (2007), and Bean (2011), who calls them "learning logs." For instance, Wirth (2008a, n.d.) has his students identify the main points of each reading, the material they found most surprising, and the material they found most confusing, including why they found certain material confusing. As mentioned in chapter 3, Wirth found that these reflections are more highly correlated with course grades ($r = .86$) than any other of the many self-regulated learning practices he assigns. The students who more regularly and thoughtfully complete these reflections perform better on all the graded assessments, including exams. This assignment induces students not only to do the readings but also to read with the purpose of finding the most important points, identifying their affective reactions to the content, and monitoring their comprehension. Wirth then collects these reflections online and uses them to inform his minilectures and student activities for the next class. He focuses on clarifying and unpacking only what his students do not understand.

Alternative wrappers for readings, videos, and podcasts are visual study tools, such as a concept map, mind map, concept circle diagram, mind/

knowledge matrix, or flowchart (see chapter 3). Compared to Wirth's reading reflections, visual study tools require the more detailed cognitive work of structuring relationships among concepts, theories, phenomena, examples, persons, events, or stages of a process. Students are truly constructing their understanding of the material and drawing an easily retrievable memory of it. While this kind of wrapper takes advantage of the power of visuals for comprehension and retention, it does not tap into affective reactions, which are also memory tools. So visual study tools may be best suited to knowledge-heavy content, such as engineering and scientific material. And while these tools should help students identify what confuses them, they do not convey this information as directly to you as does a reflective probe. You can, of course, look over the visuals your students submit and probably figure out where their understanding is breaking down. Another complication with visuals is that you need to teach your students how to make them—first by offering examples, then by having them create their own in small groups.

One other option harnesses the power of self-testing and retrieval practice, which chapter 3 discusses in some detail. Certainly, you can always give daily quizzes, but keep in mind that short-essay quizzes more effectively help students evaluate their own learning than do objective items (Sullivan, Middendorf, & Camp, 2008), and you can specs-grade them quickly. However, the easiest alternative is to let students write a mind dump during the first five or 10 minutes of class where they record everything they can remember from what they previously read, listened to, or watched. Collect these mind dumps, specs-grade them, and return them to students at the beginning of the next exam. This exercise makes students aware of what they can recall and, if you give them a minute to look at what a couple of their neighbors wrote, what they could not recall and need to relearn.

For Exams and Major Quizzes

Almost all of us give exams or major quizzes, and we can make them learning experiences rather than just student-sorting mechanisms by incorporating an exam wrapper after each one. In the next chapter, you will read about the multidisciplinary experimental studies conducted by Zimmerman and his associates that offer impressive evidence that self-regulated learning boosts student achievement. One common component across the treatment-group classes was the post-graded-exam self-assessment. In developmental mathematics, for instance, students filled in a form that asked them to evaluate how well they prepared for the quiz or exam, analyze what caused their errors, solve the quiz/exam problems they missed and similar problems successfully, explain the correct problem-solving strategy, assess their confidence to solve similar problems, and plan their study strategies for next time. In developmental writing, students completed revision sheets that posed similar questions—how students prepared for the quiz, where they went wrong, and how they planned to prepare better for the next quiz. In addition, they did something comparable to re-solving a missed problem: redoing the writing task assessed on the quiz (summarizing or paraphrasing) but on a different passage. In this classic self-regulatory activity, students were consciously learning from their mistakes—until they got it right. The second time, they usually did, with the help of their instructor, peers, or both. This approach represents a radical departure from what we typically do now, which is to mark errors as wrong, jot down an explanation that students find cryptic, and move along to the next lesson. Students are not likely to learn just by being told they are wrong.

While practically guaranteed to enhance your students' learning, this particular post-graded-exam self-assessment is not that easy to implement. You have to prepare a parallel exam with different problems, passages, questions, or items that are suitable for assessing the same skills as the original exam. In terms of class time, you have to allow enough of it for your students to correct their mistakes or redo a task with you and other students serving as advisors. Finally, you have to go over your students' exams twice, though the task should be fairly easy the second time.

If you know you can't handle this workload, you can at least provide a post-graded-exam self-assessment minus the redo component, however wise it may be to keep it. Even this streamlined self-assessment can direct students' attention to the discrepancy between their predicted and actual grades, the effectiveness of their preparation and time-management strategies, the types of items they missed, and the reasons they missed them. Chapter 6 provides specific questions and a model form.

For Major and Recurring Assignments

If much of your course revolves around a major or recurring assignment or activity, such as case debriefings, problem-based learning, a major paper or project, a portfolio, or any of the experiential learning methods (service-learning, fieldwork, an internship, a simulation, or frequent role-plays), complement that activity or method with a reflective meta-assignment (see chapter 5). If you do not, your students will not take your other self-regulated learning course components seriously. A common recurring assignment is the two- to five-page paper, often an essay, which students may or may not revise. If you attach just one meta-assignment to this kind of paper, having students write a paraphrase based off of your feedback will carry the most value. If they do not do so, most of your comments and recommendations will likely go unread or misunderstood; either way, most of the time you invested in writing them will have been a waste of time and of no help to your students. If you are having your students revise the paper, ask them further to develop a plan for the revision, stating specifically how they plan to address each concern that you or fellow students have raised.

For Closing a Course

If you normally give an essay final exam, you might as well give that same final at the beginning of the course and have students correct and rewrite it at the end of the course. Kraft (2008), Griffiths (2010), and Coggeshall (personal correspondence, 2010–11) offer somewhat different models for this approach. All that this strategy requires of you is advance planning of your final exam. Similarly, if you have your students write "How I Earned an A in This Course" at the beginning, consider having them revisit the topic at the end to evaluate their efforts. Another simple yet powerful assignment is the "Letter to the Next Cohort," in which your current students advise succeeding students on how to do well in your course—how important it is to attend class regularly, how to study, how to approach assignments, and the like—and what valuable content and skills they can learn (MacDonald, n.d.). These letters reap self-regulatory benefits for both your outgoing and your future students. Chapter 9 has details on all these techniques.

Achieving Full Integration

Courses can take different routes to become what you might call "fully integrated" with self-regulated learning. The models in the next chapter vary widely. Perkins (2008) achieves it with course portfolios that contain not only the student's content-related work but also 13 different self-regulated learning assignments done during and out of class, plus wrappers for every exam, but Wirth (2008a, n.d.) does it with a somewhat different combination of wrappers and other activities, such as learning journals. All the courses Zimmerman and his associates (2011) studied relied on frequent quizzes and exams, during which students assessed their confidence and after which they did the most extensive version of the post-graded-exam self-assessment, including redoing missed problems and faulty written work.

You have to use your own judgment about the best approach for your students, and your answers depend on your students, your subject matter, your outcomes, and how your course is delivered. For instance, in-class activities do not transfer easily to a synchronous online environment, and they don't transfer at all to an asynchronous one. If your course emphasizes solving mathematics-based problems, such as with statistics, physics, and economics, focus only on the meta-assignments and exam wrappers for this kind of problem. If the course delivers a lot of material via lecture, whether live or recorded, and your students seem not to process it well, consider some of the self-regulated learning activities and assignments for live lectures. If your students are plagued by impulsive behavior and procrastination, implement at least some of the behavior-changing strategies in chapter 8. If they complain about your course being useless or impractical, assign the "Future Uses" paper (see chapter 9).

Ease into new self-regulated learning activities and assignments after you are comfortable with your earlier choices. Accommodate your class schedule to a few, then introduce another, and a semester or two later, one more. Feel free to swap out one activity or assignment for another. As with exercise, avoid committing yourself to an agenda you cannot continue indefinitely. Expect to have to explain the learning value of each activity or assignment to your students more than once. Chances are that they have not done any of these before, and they may find them odd, even if inoffensive, at first.

The Payoff

The final chapter provides empirically based reasons why incorporating self-regulated learning activities and assignments into your courses is well worth the effort. I discuss several fully integrated courses and, for those systematically studied, document their impact on student achievement, as measured by both instructor-developed and external exams. These results reinforce the claim (Ottenhoff, 2008) that the students who are helped the most by practicing self-regulated learning are those who need help the most.

MODELS OF INTEGRATED
COURSES AND THEIR
IMPACT ON STUDENTS

We know how models can help our students learn how to write or design something new. Models can help instructors in the same way. So before you go on your own with incorporating self-regulated learning into your courses, let's study some actual examples of how other instructors have done it. Interestingly, most are in the STEM disciplines. While the following geology courses are not subjects of systematic study, the rest of them are, and they show how powerful self-regulated learning can be in raising student achievement.

Geology

Few courses are more content-rich than those in the sciences. Yet Perkins, who teaches geology, has successfully woven an array of self-regulated learning activities through his courses during the past 15 years. He calls this a *parallel curriculum* that teaches students how to learn his content curriculum (2008; personal correspondence, December 8, 2012). Following Pintrich's (2002) counsel, Perkins introduces students to the nature of learning and metacognition immediately by having them read and discuss the article he wrote with Wirth titled "Learning to Learn" (2008b), a reading recommended in chapter 2. Then he leads them through a series of self-regulatory writing assignments that they later assemble into a course learning portfolio (see the section on student portfolios in chapter 5), along with all their content-focused class activities and homework.

- A Think-Pair-Share-Write exercise on "Why are you in this class? What are your goals?" at the beginning of the course
- A course-encompassing knowledge survey and reflective essay on the subject matter at the beginning of the course
- The essay "How I Earned an A in This Course" at the beginning of the course
- Regular reflective writing on "How do I learn best?" in which students must show evidence of having experimented with, monitored, and evaluated different learning and studying methods and determined how they learn best—early in the course as well as during it
- Reflective writing on their understanding of their preferred learning styles (topic addressed in Wirth & Perkins, 2008b)
- Written evidence of their use of Bloom's taxonomy and Fink's significant learning experiences in their portfolio (topics addressed in Wirth & Perkins, 2008b)
- Written evidence of their critical thinking (topic addressed in Wirth & Perkins, 2008b)
- Written evidence of their affective learning (topic addressed in Wirth & Perkins, 2008b)
- Written evidence of their level of cognitive development, according to Perry's schema of stages (topic addressed in Wirth & Perkins, 2008b)
- Written evidence of the connections that they have observed among their commitment, the effort, and their grades (topic addressed in Wirth & Perkins, 2008b).
- Wrappers around every exam in which students predict their score and describe how they prepared before they take the exam
- A course-encompassing knowledge survey and reflective essay on the subject matter at the end of the course
- A review and critique of the course

All these assignments total to a considerable amount of work along with the task of learning geology. Yet, Perkins claims, his students apparently see the value of the assignments because they are completed without protest. As his students watch their portfolio become thicker, they have physical evidence of all that they are learning. To help his students keep up with their assignments and to underline the importance of their work, he collects and scans these portfolios every two weeks. While he has implemented his parallel curriculum mainly in small- to medium-size classes, he has adapted it to large classes as well.

Wirth (2008a; 2008b; personal correspondence, February 26, 2013) also teaches geology and infuses his courses with self-regulated learning activities and assignments, many of which echo Perkins's. His students don't seem to mind the extra work either. He, too, starts off the course by having his students read and discuss his "Learning to Learn" article (Wirth & Perkins, 2008b). Then he has them complete the following through the semester:

- A course-encompassing knowledge survey on the subject matter at the beginning of the course.
- A knowledge survey the day before an exam on the material covered by the exam to inform students how ready they are.
- The essay, "How I Earned an A in This Course," written at the beginning of the course as a letter about what they accomplished in the course.
- A midsemester progress assessment on how closely they have been following their plans in the essay.
- Explicit critical thinking practice during brief, daily class discussions on a newspaper article about its perspective, its purpose or goal, the main question it raises, the concepts and theories it espouses, the inferences it contains, the assumptions behind it, or its implications— all "elements of thought" in Paul and Elder's (2011) critical thinking framework.
- Regular reflective writing (journaling) on learning in which students describe and evaluate their strategies, modify these strategies and monitor the results, and relate their learning in this course to their learning in other courses (to encourage transfer of self-regulated learning skills). Wirth in turn advises his classes on strategies to learn more deeply.
- Regular reading reflections, each of a few hundred words, in which students write answers to two out of three questions that ask them to identify the main point, the material they found most surprising, and the material they found most confusing, including why they find certain material confusing (Wirth, n.d.).
- Reflections before each exam about the three most important points in the material on which they will be tested. Students must contribute to the online forum to gain access to the reflections of their peers.
- Preexam grade expectations and postexam reflections and error analyses.
- A course-encompassing knowledge survey on the subject matter at the end of the course.

The students' reading reflections have proven to be the self-regulated learning activity most highly correlated with their performance in daily class activities and clicker exercises and ultimately their course grades, Wirth (2008a) reports. Specifically, the more faithfully and thoughtfully students complete this assignment, the better they perform in the course. Naturally, these reflections motivate students to do the readings to begin with, but the readings are not the only source of tested content and skills. The correlation between students' reading reflections and their grade has been a startling .86, and by extrapolation, these reflections have accounted for 74% of the variance in the course grades. Following the JiTT (Just-in-TimeTeaching) method, Wirth collects his students' reading reflections online and uses them to shape his lecture and activities for the next class meeting.

Neither Perkins nor Wirth have gathered hard data on their students' performance before and after adding self-regulated learning skills to their course objectives, but both have observed that doing so has enhanced their students' content learning. The next several course examples have been the subjects of systematic research and have generated convincing results.

Developmental Mathematics

The chapters on meta-assignments (chapter 5) and quizzes and exams (chapter 6) refer to a study conducted by Zimmerman et al. (2011) in which self-regulated learning activities raised the achievement of technical college students in developmental mathematics courses. Let's look at this research more carefully.

Conducted at the New York City College of Technology (NYCCT or City Tech), the study followed a randomized experimental design involving 140 students in six different sections, three of which received traditional instruction and three of which incorporated specific self-regulated learning activities. The instructors of the latter sections first explained to their classes how errors offered learning opportunities and both modeled and provided practice in error detection and strategy adaptation. Then they gave 15- to 20-minute quizzes with four or five problems every two or three class periods. Each problem asked students not only for the solution (with all work shown) but also for a rating of their confidence in their ability to solve it before they started trying to solve it and again after solving it. The problems on the three periodic course exams, standardized across all six sections, also asked for before-and-after confidence ratings. This procedure sensitized overconfident students to their faulty self-assessments. The instructors graded and returned the quizzes quickly, either during the same class session or at the beginning of the next. Students then had the opportunity to earn back lost points by completing a self-reflection form for each missed or incomplete problem. The form had sections for them to do certain self-regulatory tasks: evaluate their quiz preparation, review and appraise their confidence ratings, analyze the sources of their errors, solve the original and a similar problem successfully, explain the appropriate problem-solving strategy, and rate their confidence to solve another similar problem. When a problem stumped them, students were urged to get help from a peer or the instructor.

The results showed that self-regulated learning activities made a marked difference in student success. Students in the sections with these activities significantly outperformed the control-group students in the second and third periodic course exams as well as the final exam. (In the first exam, there was no significant difference.) They were also significantly less overconfident in their postexam self-evaluations. In addition, a significantly higher percentage of them passed the course (68% versus 49%) and the gateway test required for admission into credit-bearing courses (64% versus 39%).

Zimmerman's team conducted a separate experimental study on students who, after failing CUNY's mathematics placement test, were enrolled in a five-week developmental math course offered in the summer. At the end, the students retook the placement test. Those in the sections infused with self-regulated learning activities passed it at a much higher rate (84%) than those in the control-group sections (63%). In addition, 60% of the former group successfully completed a credit-bearing math course the following fall, versus only 34% of the latter group. The statistically significant differences between the two groups persisted in the average number of credits earned at the college after five semesters: 34 by the former compared to 28 by the latter.

The developmental math programs at other two-year colleges—LaGuardia Community College and Raymond Walters College within the University of Cincinnati—followed NYCCT's approach, incorporated similar student activities into their classes, and realized positive results. Compared to previous sections of the course, students earned modestly but significantly higher grades and had about a 25% higher pass rate (Glenn, 2010; J. Hudesman, personal correspondence, November 26, 2012; Hudesman et al., under review).

Introductory Mathematics

While studying the effects of self-regulated learning activities on the achievement of developmental math students, Zimmerman et al. (2011) also conducted parallel research on students in introductory math courses. This latter population involved 346 students in 12 sections, six control groups and six treatment groups. This study followed the same randomized experimental design, and the students in the treatment group received the same self-regulated learning instruction, the same schedule and format of quizzes and periodic course exams, and the same postquiz reflection and correction options as students in the developmental math treatment groups. These introductory math students performed significantly better than those in the control group on all three of the periodic course exams as well as the final exam. In addition, they were significantly more accurate in their postexam self-evaluations.

Electromechanical Engineering Technology

This research project took place in NYCCT's two-year associate degree program in electromechanical engineering technology. Following Zimmerman and Hudesman's randomized pre- and posttest experimental design, the participating instructors instituted self-regulated learning activities in some sections of the electrical circuits course and the digital controls course and not in others. These activities included quizzes that probed students' confidence levels before and after solving each problem and a postquiz/postexam form for reflection and error analysis and correction. Additionally, students were asked to explain on the form why their actual performance differed from their expected score. They also had the chance to solve a similar problem to the one they missed to earn back points. Compared to those in the control-group sections, the students practicing self-regulated learning had higher course retention rates as well as higher grades on the standardized midterm and final exams. Their instructors also reported more student activity and collaboration in class and greater student emphasis on strategy selection and implementation in problem solving (Blank et al., 2006; Self-Regulated Learning Program, n.d.).

Developmental Writing

NYCCT's developmental writing faculty participated in a similar study. While the developmental writing course required different self-regulated learning activities from those in the mathematical problem-solving courses, the focus was still on identifying and correcting errors. An example of the revision sheets that the faculty developed for the major quizzes is shown in chapter 6. As you may recall, it asks students to redo the writing task that the quiz assesses and to answer questions on where they went wrong in the quiz, how they prepared for it, and how they will prepare better next time. During the five-semester project, the faculty selected about half of the sections to serve as the control group and the other half as the treatment group but did not randomize students between them. Compared to students in the former group, those in the latter quickly came to value and use the feedback they received from each other and their instructor, and they started using composition vocabulary. In addition, 18% more of them passed CUNY's writing exam than did the students in the control-group sections (Glenn, 2010).

A five-week intensive writing course was also offered in the summer to students who had failed the CUNY writing exam. Again, some sections were comprised of the control group and other sections integrated self-regulated learning activities throughout the course. When retested, only 52% of the control-group students passed the exam, while 72% of the treatment-group students passed it. In addition, only 32% of the former group successfully completed a credit-bearing writing course in the following fall semester, compared to 65% of the latter. All these group differences were highly significant (Self-Regulated Learning Program, n.d.).

Why Not Entire Programs?

Just from observing how a single course usually affects students, we can expect that the isolated efforts of one faculty member teaching two or three courses to develop learning skills might have a limited influence on students. But consider the potentially major impact of an entire program incorporating self-regulated learning outcomes in all its courses. The effect on students could be transformative. Departments might finally make good on their promise to turn out lifelong learners.

Unfortunately, we currently lack sufficient data to back up this claim. Only one program ever tried weaving self-regulated learning skills through its coursework: the College Tech Prep Program associated with Youngstown State University, a transition-to-college curriculum offered by a handful of Ohio institutions. Beginning in the 11th grade, this program is designed to lead to a certificate, apprenticeship completion, associate degree, or bachelor's degree. NYCCT's project, supported by a grant from the Fund for the Improvement of Post-Secondary Education (FIPSE), made possible a pilot faculty training program during which the teachers learned and practiced the process of goal-setting, planning, self-monitoring, and self-evaluating. They in turn used this process to design and improve self-regulated learning activities for their students. However, unlike the NYCCT faculty in the previous studies, they did not follow a strict schedule of quizzes and exams with confidence probes or postquiz/postexam reflections and corrections, nor did they collect systematic data on changes in their students' learning or performance. The project lasted only two months and yielded just a modest amount of data on the teachers' impressions of the impact of these new self-regulated learning activities. Even so, the results are worth reporting.

Initially, the teachers had little faith that these activities would have any effect on their students, but they changed their minds as they noted their classes displaying greater engagement, submitting higher-quality homework, and performing better on tests. They also reported that many of their students started practicing goal-setting, planning, self-monitoring, and self-evaluation on their own.

Still, no disciplinary major or general education program in higher education has committed itself to making self-regulated learning a distinguishing skill of its graduates. Perhaps it is time. In 2009, 75% or more of employers complained that our graduates fall short on communication skills, critical thinking and analytic reasoning skills, and the ability to analyze and solve complex problems (Hart Research Associates, 2010). Yet we in the academy swear that we are teaching those skills. If we continue teaching the same way we have been and expect better results, aren't we showing the popular sign of insanity? Given the leaps in student performance that self-regulated learning pioneers have realized, we would be wise to adopt such an effective strategy more broadly on at least an experimental basis. The monetary costs of doing so would be negligible, and the additional time burden on faculty, minimal (see chapter 10). What *would* increase is students' time-on-task, which we know is related to learning and has been declining for decades (Babcock & Marks, 2011). Fostering self-regulated learning skills may prove to be a student-friendly way to restore academic rigor in college-level courses.

REFERENCES

Academic Advising and Support Services, Loyola University, Chicago. (n.d.). Retrieved November 28, 2012, from http://www.luc.edu/advising/pdfs/pos texam_survey.pdf

Achacoso, M. V. (2004). Post-test analysis: A tool for developing students' metacognitive awareness and self-regulation. In M. V. Achacoso & M. D. Svinicki (Eds.), *New directions for teaching and learning, No. 100: Alternative strategies for evaluating student learning* (pp. 115–119). San Francisco: Jossey-Bass.

Amador, J. A., Miles, L., & Peters, C. B. (2006). *The practice of problem-based learning: A guide to implementing PBL in the classroom.* Bolton, MA: Anker.

American Association of Colleges and Universities. (2002). *Greater expectations: A new vision for learning as a nation goes to college.* Washington, DC: American Association of Colleges and Universities.

American Association of Colleges and Universities. (2007). *College learning for the new global century.* Washington, DC: American Association of Colleges and Universities.

Anderson, L. W., & Krathwohl, D. R. (2000). *A taxonomy for learning, teaching, and assessing: A revision of Bloom's Taxonomy of Educational Objectives.* Boston: Allyn & Bacon.

Anderson, R. C. (1984). Some reflection on the acquisition of knowledge. *Educational Researcher, 13*(2), 5–10.

Angelo, T. A., & Cross, P. K. (1993). *Classroom assessment techniques: A handbook for college teachers* (2nd ed.). San Francisco: Jossey-Bass.

Archintaki, D., Lewis, G. J., & Bates, T. C. (2012). Genetic influences on psychological well-being: A nationally representative twin study. *Journal of Personality, 81*(2), 221–230. doi: 10.1111/j.1467-6494.2012.00787.x. Retrieved May 27, 2012, from http://www.midus.wisc.edu/findings/pdfs/1213.pdf

Astin, A. W., Vogelgesang, L. J., Ikeda, E. K., & Yee, J. A. (2000). *How service-learning affects students.* Higher Education Research Institute, University of California, Los Angeles.

Azevedo, R., & Cromley, J. G. (2004). Does training on self-regulated learning facilitate students' learning with hypermedia? *Journal of Educational Psychology, 96*(3), 523–535.

Babcock, P., & Marks, M. (2011). The falling time cost of college: Evidence from half a century of time use data. *Review of Economics and Statistics, 93*(2), 468–478. Retrieved October 16, 2012, from http://www.mitpressjournals.org/doi/pdf/10.1162/REST_a_00093

Bandura, A. (1977). *Social learning theory.* Englewood Cliffs, NJ: Prentice-Hall.

Bandura, A. (1986). *Social foundations of thought and action: A social cognitive theory.* Englewood Cliffs, NJ: Prentice-Hall.

Bandura, A. (1997). *Self-efficacy: The exercise of control.* New York: W. H. Freeman.

Bangert-Drowns, R. L., Kulik, C.-L. C., Kulik, J. A., & Morgan, M. (1991). The instructional effect of feedback in test-like events. *Review of Educational Research, 61,* 213–238.

Barkley, E. F. (2009). *Student engagement techniques: A handbook for college faculty.* San Francisco: Jossey-Bass.

Bauerlein, M. (2008). *The dumbest generation: How the digital age stupefies young Americans and jeopardizes our future.* New York: Tarcher/Penguin.

Baxter Magolda, M. B. (1992). *Knowing and reasoning in college: Gender-related patterns in students' intellectual development.* San Francisco: Jossey-Bass.

Bean, J. C. (2011). *Engaging ideas: The professor's guide to integrating writing, critical thinking, and active learning in the classroom* (2nd ed.). San Francisco: Jossey-Bass.

Bell, P., & Volckmann, D. (2011). Knowledge surveys in general chemistry: Confidence, overconfidence, and performance. *Journal of Chemical Education, 88*(11), 1469–1476. doi: 10.1021/ed100328c

Bembenutty, H. (2011). Academic delay of gratification and academic achievement. In H. Bembenutty (Ed.), *New directions for teaching and learning, No. 126: Self-regulated learning* (pp. 55–65). San Francisco: Jossey-Bass.

Bergmann, J., & Sams, A. (2012). *Flip your classroom: Reach every student in every class every day.* Washington, DC: International Society for Technology in Education.

Berrett, D. (2012, January 17). Note to faculty: Don't be such a know-it-all. *Chronicle of Higher Education.* Retrieved January 18, 2012, from http://chronicle.com/article/Note-to-Faculty-Dont-Be-Such/130374/?sid=at&utm_source=at&utm_medium=en

Blank, S., Hudesman, J., Morton, E., Armstrong, R., Moylan, A., White, N., & Zimmerman, B. J. (2006). A self-regulated learning assessment system for electromechanical engineering technology students. Presented at the *Proceedings of the National STEM Assessment Conference,* (pp. 37–45). Retrieved November 28, 2012, from http://openwatermedia.com/downloads/STEM(for-posting).pdf#page=41

Bligh, D. A. (2000). *What's the use of lectures?* San Francisco: Jossey-Bass.

Bloom, B. (1968). Learning for mastery. *Evaluation Comment, 1*(2), 1–12.

Bloom, B. (1971). Mastery learning. In J. H. Block (Ed.), *Mastery learning: Theory and practice* (pp. 47–63). New York: Holt, Rinehart & Winston.

Bloom, B., & Associates. (1956). *Taxonomy of educational objectives.* New York: David McKay.

Bonwell, C. C., & Eison, J. A. (1991). *Active learning: Creating excitement in the classroom.* (ASHE-ERIC Higher Education Report No. 1). Washington, DC: George Washington University, School of Education and Human Development.

Boud, D. (1995). *Enhancing learning through self-assessment.* London: Kogan Page.

Boud, D. (2000). Sustainable assessment: Rethinking assessment for the learning society. *Studies in Continuing Education, 22*(2), 151–167.

Boud, D., & Falchikov, N. (1989). Quantitative studies of student self-assessment in higher education: A critical analysis of findings. *Higher Education, 18*, 529–549.

Bowen, J. A. (2012). *Teaching naked: How moving technology out of your college classroom will improve student learning.* San Francisco: Jossey-Bass.

Bradley, R. T., McCraty, R., Atkinson, M., Tomasino, D., Daughterty, A., & Auguelles, L. (2010). Emotion self-regulation, psychophysiological coherence, and test anxiety: Results from an experiment using electrophysiological measures. *Applied Physiology and Biofeedback, 35*(4), 261–283. doi: 10.1007/s10484-010-9134-x

Bransford, J. D., Brown, A. L., & Cocking, A. R. (2000). *How people learn: Brain, mind, experience, and school.* Washington, DC: National Research Council, National Academy Press.

Brown, R., & Pressley, M. (1994). Self-regulated learning and getting meaning from text: The Transactional Strategies Instruction model and its ongoing validation. In D. H. Schunk & B. J. Zimmerman (Eds.), *Self-regulation of learning and performance: Issues and Educational Applications* (pp. 155–180). Hillsdale, NJ: Erlbaum.

Brown, T., Kraft, K., Yu, S., Alabi, W., McGuire, S., & Myers, J. (2008, November). *Early warning.* Session presented at the National Association of Geoscience Teachers (NAGT) Workshops: The Role of Metacognition in Teaching Geoscience, Carleton College, Northfield, MN. Retrieved December 30, 2011, from http://serc.carleton.edu/NAGTWorkshops/metacognition/group_tactics/28891.html

Brown, T., & Rose, B. (2008, November). *Use of metacognitive wrappers for field experiences.* Session presented at the National Association of Geoscience Teachers (NAGT) Workshops: The Role of Metacognition in Teaching Geoscience, Carleton College, Northfield, MN. Retrieved December 30, 2011, from http://serc.carleton.edu/NAGTWorkshops/metacognition/tactics/28926.html

Burns, D. D. (1989). *The feeling good handbook.* New York: William Morrow & Company.

Butler, A. C. (2010). Repeated testing produces superior transfer of learning relative to repeated studying. *Journal of Experimental Psychology: Learning, Memory, and Cognition, 36*, 716–727.

Butler, D. L., & Winne, P. H. (1995). Feedback and self-regulated learning: A theoretical synthesis. *Review of Educational Research, 65*, 245–282.

Catalano, R. F., Haggerty, K. P., Gainey, R. R., & Hoppe, M. J. (1979). Reducing parental risk factor for children's substance misuse: Preliminary outcomes with opiate-addicted parents. *Substance Abuse and Misuse, 32*(6), 699–721.

Center for Academic Success, Louisiana State University. (2010). *The study cycle.* Retrieved February 15, 2012, from https://cas.lsu.edu/sites/cas.lsu.edu/files/attachments/LL4%20Study%20Cycle%202010.pdf

Cobern, W. W., & Loving, C. C. (1998). The card exchange: Introducing the philosophy of science. In W. F. McComas (Ed.), *The nature of science in science education: Rationales and strategies* (pp. 73–82). Dordrecht, The Netherlands: Kluwer.

Colvin, G. (2008). *Talent is overrated: What really separates world-class performers from everybody else.* New York: Penguin Group.

Cooper, M. M., & Sandi-Urena, S. (2009). Design and validation of an instrument to assess metacognitive skillfulness in chemistry problem solving. *Journal of Chemical Education, 86*(2), 240–245. Available at http://pubs.acs.org/doi/abs/10.1021/ed086p240

Costa, A. L., & Kallick, B. (2000). Getting into the habit of reflection. *Educational Leadership, 57*(7), 60–62.

Cuseo, J. B. (2002). *Igniting student involvement, peer interaction, and teamwork.* Stillwater, OK: New Forums Press.

Davidson, C. (2009, July 26). How to crowdsource grading. HASTAC blog. Retrieved April 25, 2013, from http://hastac.org/blogs/cathy-davidson/how-crowdsource-grading

Davidson, R. J. (2003). Affective neuroscience and psychophysiology: Toward a synthesis. *Psychophysiology, 40,* 655–665.

Davis, G. R. (2012). *Syllabus for BIO 342: Human Physiology, Wofford University.* Retrieved December 15, 2012, from http://webs.wofford.edu/davisgr/bio342/index.htm

Davis, S. F., & Palladino, J. J. (2002). *Psychology* (3rd ed.). Upper Saddle River, NJ: Prentice-Hall.

Delclos, V. R., & Harrington, C. (1991). Effects of strategy monitoring and proactive instruction on children's problem-solving performance. *Journal of Educational Psychology, 83,* 35-42.

Demet, Z., Sook, J., Gertrude, S., Perkins, D., Meyers, J., Lea, P., . . . Sablock, J. (2008, November). *Using a problem-based learning approach to help students learn how experts solve problems.* Session presented at the National Association of Geoscience Teachers (NAGT) Workshops: The Role of Metacognition in Teaching Geoscience, Carleton College, Northfield, MN. Retrieved January 16, 2012, from http://serc.carleton.edu/NAGTWorkshops/metacognition/tactics/28930.html

Duckworth, A., Peterson, C., Matthews, M., & Kelly, D. (2007). Grit: The perseverance and passion for long-term goals. *Journal of Personality and Social Psychology, 92*(6), 1087–1101.

Duckworth, A., & Seligman, M. (2005). Self-discipline outdoes IQ in predicting academic performance of adolescents. *Psychological Science, 16*(12), 939–944.

Duke, R. A., Simmons, A. L., & Cash, C. D. (2009). It's not how much; it's how: Characteristics of practice behavior and retention of performance skills. *Journal of Research in Music Education, 56*(4), 310–321. doi: 10.1177/0022429408328851

Duncan, N. (2007). Feed-forward: Improving students' use of tutors' comments. *Assessment & Evaluation in Higher Education, 32*(2), 271–283.

Dweck, C. S. (2007). *Mindset: The new psychology of success.* New York: Random House.

Edens, K. M. (2000). Preparing problem solvers for the 21st century through problem-based learning. *College Teaching, 48*(2), 55–60.

Edwards, N. (2007). Student self-grading in social statistics. *College Teaching, 55*(2), 72–76.

Edwards, R. K., Kellner, K. R., Sistrom, C. L., & Magyari, E. J. (2003). Medical student self-assessment of performance on an obstetrics and gynecology clerkship. *American Journal of Obstetrics and Gynecology, 188*(4), 1078–1082.

Elliott, D. (2010, August 1). How to teach the trophy generation. *Chronicle of Higher Education.* Retrieved January 18, 2012, from http://chronicle.com/article/How -to-Teach-the-Trophy/123723/?sid=pm&utm_source=pm&utm_medium=en

Ericsson, K. A., Krampe, R. T., & Tesch-Römer, C. (1993). The role of deliberate practice in the acquisition of expert performance. *Psychological Review, 100*(3), 363–406. doi: 10.1037/0033-295X.100.3.363

Evans, G. W., & Rosenbaum, J. (2008). Self-regulation and the income-achievement gap. *Early Childhood Research Quarterly, 23*(4), 504–514. doi: 10.1016/j. ecresq.2008.07.002

Eyler, J., & Giles, D. E., Jr. (1999). *Where's the learning in service-learning?* San Francisco: Jossey-Bass.

Falchikov, N., & Boud, D. (1989). Student self-assessment in higher education: A meta-analysis. *Review of Educational Research, 59*(4), 395–430.

Fink, L. D. (2003). *Creating significant learning experiences: An integrated approach to designing college courses.* San Francisco: Jossey-Bass.

Fuchs, A. H. (1997). Ebbinghaus's contributions to psychology after 1885. *American Journal of Psychology, 110*(4), 621–634.

Fuhrman, M., King, H., Ludwig, M., & Johnston, J. (2008, November). *A gateway metacognitive tactic for "busy" faculty.* Session presented at the National Association of Geoscience Teachers (NAGT) Workshops: The Role of Metacognition in Teaching Geoscience, Carleton College, Northfield, MN. Retrieved January 15, 2012, from http://serc.carleton.edu/NAGTWorkshops/metacognition/group _tactics/28903.html

Garner, R., & Alexander, P. A. (1989). Metacognition: Answered and unanswered questions. *Educational Psychologist, 24,* 143–158.

Garrett, D. (2012, February). *Help students make better decisions by understanding the neuroscience of procrastination.* Session presented at the annual Lilly South Conference on College Teaching, Greensboro, NC.

Gatta, L. A. (1973). An analysis of the pass-fail grading system as compared to the conventional grading system in high school chemistry. *Journal of Research in Science Teaching, 10*(1), 3–12.

Glenn, D. (2010, February 7). How students can improve by studying themselves. *Chronicle of Higher Education.* Retrieved March 12, 2010, from http://chronicle .com/article/Struggling-Students-Can-Imp/64004/

Goleman, D. (1996). *Working with emotional intelligence: Why it can matter more than IQ.* London: Bloomsbury.

Griffiths, E. (2010). Clearing the misty landscape: Teaching students what they didn't know then, but know now. *College Teaching, 58*(1), 3–37.

Gronlund, N. E., & Waugh, C. K. (2009). *Assessment of student achievement* (9th ed.). Needham Heights, MA: Allyn & Bacon.

Grossman, R. (2009). Structures for facilitating student reflection. *College Teaching, 57*(1), 15–22.

Hart Research Associates on behalf of the Association of American Colleges and Universities. (2010). *Raising the bar: Employers' views on college learning in the wake of the economic downturn.* Retrieved November 26, 2012, from http://www.aacu.org/leap/documents/2009_EmployerSurvey.pdf

Hattie, J. (2009). The black box of tertiary assessment: An impending revolution. In L. H. Meyer, S. Davidson, H. Anderson, R. Fletcher, P. M. Johnston, & M. Rees (Eds.), *Tertiary assessment and higher education student outcomes: Policy, practice and research* (pp. 259–275). Wellington, NZ: Ako Aotearoa.

Hattie, J., & Timperley, H. (2007). The power of feedback. *Review of Educational Research, 77*(1), 81–112. Retrieved April 23, 2012, from http://rer.sagepub.com/content/77/1/81.full

Hazard, L. L. (1997). *The effect of locus of control and attitudes toward intelligence on study habits of college students.* Unpublished doctoral dissertation, Boston University.

Hazard, L. L. (2011). Time management, motivation, and procrastination: Understanding and teaching students self-regulatory behaviors. *Innovative Educators* webinar broadcast live and recorded November 4.

Hazard, L. L., & Nadeau, J. (2012). *Foundations for learning* (3rd ed.). Upper Saddle River, NJ: Prentice-Hall.

Hofer, B., Yu, S., & Pintrich, P. R. (1998). Teaching college students to be self-regulated learners. In D. H. Schunk & B. J. Zimmerman (Eds.), *Self-regulated learning: From teaching to self-reflective practice* (pp. 57–85). New York: Guilford.

Hudesman, J., Crosby, S., Isaac, S., Flugman, B., Clay, D., & Everson, H. (Under review). *The dissemination of an enhanced formative assessment and self-regulated learning program to improve student achievement in developmental mathematics.* Manuscript submitted for publication.

Husman, J. (2008, November). *Self-regulation is more than metacognition.* Keynote address presented at the National Association of Geoscience Teachers (NAGT) Workshops: The Role of Metacognition in Teaching Geoscience, Carleton College, Northfield, MN. Retrieved January 16, 2012, from http://serc.carleton.edu/NAGTWorkshops/metacognition/husman.html

Immordino-Yang, M. H., & Damasio, A. (2007). We feel, therefore we learn: The relevance of affective and social neuroscience to education. *Mind, Brain, and Education, 1*(1), 3–10.

Isaacson, R. M., & Was, C. A. (2010). Building a metacognitive curriculum: An educational psychology to teach metacognition. *National Teaching & Learning Forum, 19*(5), 1–4.

Jacobs, L. C., & Chase, C. I. (1992). *Developing and using tests effectively: A guide for faculty.* San Francisco: Jossey-Bass.

Jaschik, S. (2010, May 3). No grading, more learning. *Inside Higher Education.* Retrieved May 5, 2010, from http://www.insidehighered.com/news/2010/05/03/grading

Jenson, J. D. (2011). Promoting self-regulation and critical reflection through writing students' use of electronic portfolio. *International Journal of ePortfolio, 1*(1), 49–60.

Johnson, C. I., & Mayer, R. E. (2009). A testing effect with multimedia learning. *Journal of Educational Psychology, 101,* 621–629.

Johnson, D. W., Johnson, R. T., & Smith, K. A. (1991). *Active learning: Cooperation in the college classroom.* Edina, MN: Interaction Books.

Johnston, S., & Cooper, J. (1997). Quick-thinks: The interactive lecture. *Cooperative Learning and College Teaching, 8*(1), 1–8.

Kalman, C. S. (2007). *Successful science and engineering teaching in colleges and universities.* Bolton, MA: Anker.

Karabenick, S. A., & Dembo, M. H. (2011). Understanding and facilitating self-regulated help-seeking. In H. Bembenutty (Ed.), *New directions for teaching and learning, No. 126: Self-regulated learning* (pp. 33–43). San Francisco: Jossey-Bass.

Karlins, M., Kaplan, M., & Stuart, W. (1969). Academic attitudes and performance as a function of differential grading systems: An evaluation of Princeton's pass-fail system. *Journal of Experimental Education, 37*(3), 38–50. Retrieved April 2, 2010, from http://www.jstor.org/stable/20157034

Kitsantas, A., & Zimmerman, B. J. (2009). College students' homework and academic achievement: The mediating role of self-regulatory beliefs. *Metacognitive Learning, 4,* 97–110.

Kolb, D. A. (1984). *Experiential learning: Experience as the source of learning and development.* Englewood Cliffs, NJ: Prentice-Hall.

Kraft, K. (2008, November). *Using situated metacognition to enhance student understanding of the nature of science.* Session presented at the National Association of Geoscience Teachers (NAGT) Workshops: The Role of Metacognition in Teaching Geoscience, Carleton College, Northfield, NM. Retrieved January 17, 2012, from http://serc.carleton.edu/NAGTWorkshops/metacognition/kraft.html

Kruger, J., & Dunning, D. (1999). Unskilled and unaware of it: How difficulties in recognizing one's own incompetence lead to inflated self-assessments. *Journal of Personality and Social Psychology, 77,* 1121–1134.

Kruger, J., & Dunning, D. (2002). Unskilled and unaware—but why? *Journal of Personality and Social Psychology, 82*(2), 189–192.

Kuhn, D., Schauble, L., & Garcia-Mila, M. (1992). Cross-domain development of scientific reasoning. *Cognition and Instruction, 9,* 285–327.

Kulik, C., Kulik, J., & Bangert-Drowns, R. (1990). Effectiveness of mastery learning programs: A meta-analysis. *Review of Educational Research, 60*(2), 265–306.

Kunkel, S. W. (2002). Consultant learning: A model for student-directed learning in management education. *Journal of Management Education, 26*(2), 121–138.

Lancaster, L. C., & Stillman, D. (2003). *When generations collide: Who they are. Why they clash. How to solve the generation puzzle at work.* New York: Harper Paperbacks.

Landsberger, J. (1996–2012). *Learning to learn: Metacognition.* Retrieved April 11, 2012, from http://www.studygs.net/metacognition.htm (text version at http://www.studygs.net/metacognitiona.htm)

Lang, J. M. (2012, January 17). Metacognition and student learning. *Chronicle of Higher Education.* Retrieved January 18, 2012, from http://chronicle.com/article/MetacognitionStudent/130327/?sid=at&utm_source=at&utm_medium=en

Lasry, N. (2008). Clickers or flashcards: Is there really a difference? *Physics Teacher, 46,* 242–244.

Leamnson, R. (2002). *Learning (your first job).* Retrieved December 6, 2012, from http://www.udel.edu/CIS/106/iaydin/07F/misc/firstJob.pdf

Learning Centre, The. (2008). *Reflective writing.* University of New South Wales. Retrieved March 12, 2010, from http://www.lc.unsw.edu.au/onlib/reflect.html

Leff, L. L. (n.d.). *Contract grading in teaching computer programming.* Retrieved March 20, 2010, from http://www.wiu.edu/users/mflll/GRADCONT.HTM

Lieux, E. M. (1996). Comparison study of learning in lecture vs. problem-based format. *About Teaching, 50*(1), 18–19.

Lloyd, D. A. (1992). Commentary: Pass-fail grading fails to meet the grade. *Academic Medicine, 67*(9), 583–584.

Lochhead, J., & Whimbey, A. (1987). Teaching analytical reasoning through thinking aloud pair problem solving. In J. E. Stice (Ed.), *New directions for teaching and learning, No 30: Developing critical thinking and problem solving abilities* (pp. 73–92). San Francisco: Jossey-Bass.

Longhurst, N., & Norton, L. S. (1997). Self-assessment in coursework essays. *Studies in Educational Evaluation, 23*(4), 319–330.

Lovett, M. C. (2008, January). *Teaching metacognition.* Presented at the annual meeting of the Educause Learning Initiative (ELI), San Antonio, TX. Retrieved March 11, 2010, from http://net.educause.edu/upload/presentations/ELI081/FS03/Metacognition-ELI.pdf

MacDonald, L. T. (n.d.). Letter to next term's students. *On Course Newsletter.* Retrieved April 23, 2012, from http://www.oncourseworkshop.com/Staying%20On%20Course004.htm

Mānoa Writing Program. (n.d.). *Writing Matters #5: Helping students make connections: A self-assessment approach.* University of Hawai'i at Mānoa. Retrieved March 11, 2010, from http://mwp01.mwp.hawaii.edu/resources/wm5.htm

Masui, C., & de Corte, E. (2005). Learning to reflect and to attribute constructively as basic components of self-regulated learning. *British Journal of Educational Psychology, 75,* 351–372.

Mayer, R. E. (2005). Introduction to multimedia learning. In R. E. Mayer (Ed.), *The Cambridge handbook of multimedia learning* (pp. 1–15). New York: Cambridge University Press.

Mazur, E. (1997). *Peer instruction: A user's manual.* Upper Saddle Creek, NJ: Prentice Hall.

McClure, N. C. (2005). *Demonstrated the importance and significance of the subject matter background.* POD-IDEA Center Notes on Instruction, Item #4. Manhattan, KS: The IDEA Center. Retrieved February 27, 2012, from http://www.theideacenter.org/sites/default/files/Item4Formatted.pdf

McCraty, R., & Tomasino, D. (2006). Emotional stress, positive emotions, and psychophysiological coherence. In B. B. Arnetz & R. Ekman (Eds.), *Stress in health and disease* (pp. 360–383). Weinheim, Germany: Wiley-VCH.

McDaniel, M. A., Howard, D. C., & Einstein, G. O. (2009). The Read-Recite-Review study strategy: Effective and portable. *Psychological Science, 20*(4), 516–522.

McDonald, B., & Boud, D. (2003). The impact of self-assessment on achievement: The effects of self-assessment training on performance in external examinations. *Assessment in Education, 10*(2), 209–220.

McGuire, S. (2008, November). *Using metacognition to effect an extreme academic makeover in students.* Session presented at the National Association of Geoscience Teachers (NAGT) Workshops: The Role of Metacognition in Teaching Geoscience, Carleton College, Northfield, MN. Retrieved January 17, 2012, from http://serc.carleton.edu/NAGTWorkshops/metacognition/mcguire.html

McGuire, S., Gosselin, D., Mamo, M., Holmes, M. A., Husman, J., & Rutherford, S. (2008, November). *Metacognitive learning strategies in all classes.* Session presented at the National Association of Geoscience Teachers (NAGT) Workshops: The Role of Metacognition in Teaching Geoscience, Carleton College, Northfield, MN. Retrieved January 15, 2012, from http://serc.carleton.edu/NAGTWorkshops/metacognition/tactics/28931.html

Mezeske, B. (2009). *The Graduate* revisited: Not "plastics" but "metacognition." *The Teaching Professor, 23*(9), 1.

Miller, T. M., & Geraci, L. (2011, January 24). Unskilled but aware: Reinterpreting overconfidence in low-performing students. *Journal of Experimental Psychology: Learning, Memory, and Cognition.* Advance online publication. doi: 10.1037/a0021802

Mischel, W., & Ayduk, O. (2002). Self-regulation in a cognitive-affective personality system: Attentional control in the service of the self. *Self and Identity, 1*(2), 113–120. doi: 10.1080/152988602317319285

Mischel, W., Shoda, Y., & Peake, P. (1988). The nature of adolescent competencies predicted by preschool delay of gratification. *Journal of Personality and Social Psychology, 54,* 687–696.

Mischel, W., Shoda, Y., & Rodriguez, M. L. (1989). Delay of gratification in children. *Science, 244,* 933–938.

Nathan, R. (2005). *My freshman year: What a professor learned by becoming a student.* Ithaca, NY: Cornell University Press.

Nicol, D. J., & Macfarlane-Dick, D. (2006). Formative assessment and self-regulated learning: A model and seven principles of good feedback practice. *Studies in Higher Education, 32*(2), 199–218.

Nilson, L. B. (2007). *The graphic syllabus and the outcomes map: Communicating your course.* San Francisco: Jossey-Bass.

Nilson, L. B. (2010). *Teaching at its best: A research-based resource for college instructors* (3rd ed.). San Francisco: Jossey-Bass.

Novak, J. D., & Gowin, B. D. (1984). *Learning how to learn.* Cambridge, UK: Cambridge University Press.

Nuhfer, E. B. (1996). The place of formative evaluations in assessment and ways to reap their benefits. *Journal of Geoscience Education, 44,* 385–394.

Nuhfer, E. B., & Knipp, D. (2003). The knowledge survey: A tool for all reasons. In C. Wehlburg & S. Chadwick-Blossey (Eds.), *To improve the academy. Resources for faculty, instructional, and organizational development, Vol. 21* (pp. 59–78). Boston, MA: Anker.

O'Grady, P. (2012). The Twitter generation: Teaching deferred gratification to college students. *National Teaching & Learning Forum, 21*(3), 6–8.

Orsmond, P., Merry, S., & Reiling, K. (2000). The use of student-derived marking criteria in peer and self-assessment. *Assessment and Evaluation in Higher Education, 25*(1), 23–38.

Ory, J. C., & Ryan, K. E. (1993). *Survival skills for college, Vol. 4: Tips for improving testing and grading.* Thousand Oaks, CA: Sage.

Ottenhoff, J. (2008, November). *Discussing metacognition: Metacognition, discussion boards, and the bard.* Session presented at the National Association of Geoscience Teachers (NAGT) Workshops: The Role of Metacognition in Teaching Geoscience, Carleton College, Northfield, MN. Retrieved January 17, 2012, from http://serc.carleton.edu/NAGTWorkshops/metacognition/ottenhoff.html

Ottenhoff, J. (2011). Learning how to learn: Metacognition in liberal education. *Liberal Education, 97*(3/4). Retrieved April 11, 2012, from http://www.aacu.org/liberaleducation/le-sufa11/ottenhoff.cfm?utm_source=pubs&utm_medium=blast&utm_campaign=libedsufa2011

Pacquette, L. (2011). The skills grid. *National Teaching & Learning Forum, 21*(2), 6–7.

Pasupathi, M. (2012). *How we learn.* The Great Courses, Course No. 1691. Chantilly, VA: Teaching Company.

Paul, R., & Elder, L. (2011). *The analysis and assessment of thinking.* Foundation for Critical Thinking. Retrieved November 28, 2012, from http://www.criticalthinking.org/pages/the-analysis-amp-assessment-of-thinking/497

Paulson, D. R. (1999). Active learning and cooperative learning in the organic chemistry lecture class. *Journal of Chemical Education, 76*(8), 1136–1140.

Peirce, W. (2006). *Strategies for teaching critical reading.* Retrieved December 19, 2008, from http://academic.pg.cc.md.us/~wpeirce/MCCCTR/critread.html

Perkins, D. (2008, November). *Learning portfolios and metacognition.* Session presented at the National Association of Geoscience Teachers (NAGT) Workshops: The Role of Metacognition in Teaching Geoscience, Carleton College, Northfield, MN. Retrieved January 17, 2012, from http://serc.carleton.edu/NAGTWorkshops/metacognition/perkins.html

Perry, W. G. (1968). *Forms of intellectual and ethical development in the college years: A scheme.* New York: Holt, Rinehart & Winston.

Pintrich, P. R. (2002). The role of metacognitive knowledge in learning, teaching, and assessing. *Theory into Practice, 41*(4), 219–225.

Pintrich, P. R., McKeachie, W. J., & Lin, Y. (1987). Teaching a course in learning to learn. *Teaching of Psychology, 14,* 81–86.

Pressley, M., & Ghatala, E. S. (1990). Self-regulated learning: Monitoring learning from text. *Educational Psychologist, 25,* 19–33.

Pryor, J. H., Hurtado, S., DeAngelo, L., Palucki Blake, L., & Tran, S. (2011). *The American freshman: National norms fall 2010.* Los Angeles: Higher Education Research Institute, University of California, Los Angeles.

Resnick, M. D., Harris, L. J., & Blum, R. W. (1993). Caring and connectedness in adolescent health and well-being. *Journal of Paediatrics and Child Health, 29*(1), S3–S9.

Rhem, J. (1995). Going deep. *National Teaching & Learning Forum, 5*(1). Retrieved December 21, 2009, from http://www.ntlf.com/html/pi/9512/article2.htm

Rhem, J. (2011). Laura Gibbs: Online course lady. *National Teaching & Learning Forum, 21*(1), 1–5.

Rhode Island Diploma System. (2005). *Exhibition toolkit: Support student self-management and reflection.* Retrieved January 15, 2012, from http://www.ride.ri.gov/highschoolreform/dslat/exhibit/exhact_1003.shtml#t

Robins, L. S., Fantone, J. C., Oh, M. S., Alexander, G. L., Shlafer, M., & Davis, W. K. (1995). The effect of pass/fail grading and weekly quizzes on first-year students' performances and satisfaction. *Academic Medicine 70*(4), 327–329.

Roediger, H. L., III, & Butler, A. C. (2010). The critical role of retrieval practice in long-term retention. *Trends in Cognitive Sciences, 15*(1), 20–27. doi: 10.1016/j.tics.2010.09.003

Roediger, H. L., III, & Karpicke, J. D. (2006). The power of testing memory: Basic research and implications of the educational practice. *Perspectives on Psychological Science, 1*(3), 181–210. doi: 10.1111/j.1745-6916.2006.00012.x

Rohe, D. E., Barrier, P.A., & Clark, M. M. (2006). *The benefits of pass-fail grading on stress, mood, and group cohesion in medical school.* Retrieved April 2, 2010, from http://www.mayoclinicproceedings.com/content/81/11/1443.ful

Rohrer, D., Taylor, K., & Sholar, B. (2010). Tests enhance the transfer of learning. *Journal of Experimental Psychology: Learning, Memory, and Cognition, 36*(1), 233–239. Retrieved February 25, 2012, from http://uweb.cas.usf.edu/~drohrer/pdfs/Rohrer_et_al_2010JEPLMC.pdf

Rolf, J. S., Scharff, L., & Hodge, T. (2012, January). *Does "thinking about thinking" impact completion rates of pre-class assignments?* Session presented at the Joint Math Meetings of the Mathematical Association of America and the American Mathematical Society, Boston, MA.

Rose, B., Sablock, J., Jones, F., Mogk, D., Wenk, L., & Davis, L. L. (2008, November). *A scholarly approach to critical reasoning of the geosciences literature.* Session presented at the National Association of Geoscience Teachers (NAGT) Workshops: The Role of Metacognition in Teaching Geoscience, Carleton College, Northfield, MN. Retrieved January 15, 2012, from http://serc.carleton.edu/NAGTWork shops/metacognition/group_tactics/28890.html

Ruohoniemi, M., & Lindblom-Ylänne, S. (2009). Students' experiences concerning course workload and factors enhancing and impeding their learning—a useful resource for quality enhancement in teaching and curriculum planning. *International Journal for Academic Development, 14*(1), 69–81.

Samson, P. (2008, November). *MegaCognition: Metacognition for large classes.* Session presented at the National Association of Geoscience Teachers (NAGT) Workshops: The Role of Metacognition in Teaching Geoscience, Carleton College, Northfield, MN. Retrieved January 18, 2012, from http://serc.carleton.edu/ NAGTWorkshops/metacognition/samson.html

Samson, P., Sibley, D., Briles, C., McGraw, J., Jones F., & Brassell, S. (2008, November). *A tactic to actively promote metacognitive skills as learning strategies in classroom activities using LectureTools.* Session presented at the National Association of Geoscience Teachers (NAGT) Workshops: The Role of Metacognition in Teaching Geoscience, Carleton College, Northfield, MN. Retrieved January 16, 2012, from http://serc .carleton.edu/NAGTWorkshops/metacognition/tactics/28934.html

Savin Baden, M., & Major, C. H. (2004). *Foundations of problem-based learning.* Berkshire, UK: Society for Research into Higher Education and Open University Press.

Schell, J. (2012, September 4). How one professor motivated students to read before a flipped class, and measured their effort. Turn to Your Neighbor blog. Retrieved September 8, 2012, from http://blog.peerinstruction.net/2012/09/04/how -one-professor-motivated-students-to-read-before-a-flipped-class-and-measured -their-effort/

Schoenfeld, A. H. (2010). *How we think: A theory of goal-oriented decision making and its educational applications.* New York: Routledge.

Schraw, G. (1998). Promoting general metacognitive awareness. *Instructional Science, 26,* 113–125. Retrieved March 12, 2010, from http://www.springerlink .com/content/w884l0214g78445h/

Schraw, G., & Dennison, R. S. (1994). Assessing metacognitive awareness. *Contemporary Educational Psychology, 19,* 460–475. Available through http://wiki .biologyscholars.org/@api/deki/files/99/=Schraw1994.pdf

Schunk, D. H. (1989). Self-efficacy and achievement behaviors. *Educational Psychology Review, 1,* 173–208.

Schunk, D. H., & Zimmerman, B. J. (Eds.). (1998). *Self-regulated learning: From teaching to self-reflective practice.* New York: Guilford Press.

Schwartz, B., & Sharpe, K. (2012, February 19). Colleges should teach intellectual virtues. *Chronicle of Higher Education.* Retrieved February 20, 2012, from http:// chronicle.com/article/Colleges-Should-Teach/130868/

Schwarzmueller, A. (2010, February). *Engaging students in reflecting on their learning.* Session presented at the annual Lilly South Conference on College Teaching, Greensboro, NC. Available at https://blackboard.uncg.edu/bbcswebdav/xid -1494725_1

Self-Regulated Learning Program, The. (n.d.). The Self-Regulated Learning Program (blog; multiple contributors). Retrieved November 23, 2012, from http:// www.selfregulatedlearning.blogspot.com/

Shoda, Y., Mischel, W., & Peake, P. (1990). Predicting adolescent cognitive and social competence from preschool delay of gratification: Identifying diagnostic conditions. *Developmental Psychology, 26,* 489–493.

Siegler, R. S., & Jenkins, E. (1989). *How children discover new strategies.* Hillsdale, NJ: Erlbaum.

Singleton-Jackson, J. A., Jackson, D. L., & Reinhardt, J. (2010). Students as consumers of knowledge: Are they buying what we're selling? *Innovative Higher Education, 35*(4), 343–358.

Sluijsmans, D., Dochy, F., & Moerkerke, G. (1999). Creating a learning environment by using self-, peer-, and co-assessment. *Learning Environments Research, 1,* 293–319.

Soloman, B. A., & Felder, R. M. (n.d.). *Index of Learning Styles questionnaire.* Retrieved February 1, 2012, from http://www.engr.ncsu.edu/learningstyles/ilsweb.html

Stallings, W. M., & Smock, R. (1971). The pass-fail grading option at a state university: A five-semester evaluation. *Journal of Educational Measurement, 8*(3), 153–160. Retrieved April 2, 2010, from http://www.jstor.org/stable/1434384

Steel, P. (2007). The nature of procrastination: A meta-analytic and theoretical review of quintessential self-regulatory failure. *Psychological Bulletin, 133*(1), 65–94. doi: 10.1037/0033-2909.133.1.65

Stern, L. E., & Solomon, A. (2006). Effective faculty feedback: The road less traveled. *Assessing Writing, 11,* 22–41. Retrieved April 23, 2012, from http://www.sciencedirect.com/science/article/pii/S1075293505000656

Stevens, D. D., & Levi, A. J. (2005). *Introduction to rubrics: An assessment tool to save grading time, convey effective feedback, and promote student learning.* Sterling, VA: Stylus.

Sullivan, C. S., Middendorf, J., & Camp, M. E. (2008). Engrained study habits and the challenge of warm-ups in just-in-time teaching. *National Teaching & Learning Forum, 17*(4), 5–8.

Suskie, L. (2004). *Assessing student learning: A common sense guide.* San Francisco: Jossey-Bass.

Svinicki, M. (2004). *Learning and motivation in postsecondary classrooms.* San Francisco: Jossey-Bass.

Tai-Seale, T. (2001). Liberating service-learning and applying new practice. *College Teaching, 49*(1), 14–18.

Tinnesz, C. G., Ahuna, K. H., & Kiener, M. (2006). Toward college success: Internalizing active and dynamic strategies. *College Teaching, 54*(4), 302–306.

Tough, P. (2012). *How children succeed: Grit, curiosity, and the hidden power of character.* New York: Houghton Mifflin Harcourt.

Twenge, J. M. (2007). *Generation me: Why today's young Americans are more confident, assertive, entitled and more miserable than ever before.* New York: Free Press.

University of Minnesota Libraries in collaboration with the Center for Writing. (2011). *Assignment calculator: You can be the clock.* Retrieved January, 19, 2012, from http://www.lib.umn.edu/help/calculator/

Vekiri, I. (2002). What is the value of graphical displays in learning? *Educational Psychology Review, 14*(3), 261–312. Retrieved December 1, 2010, from http://deepblue.lib.umich.edu/bitstream/2027.42/44453/1/10648_2004_Article_374334.pdf

Venditti, P. (2010, June 10). Re: End of semester sanity strategies? Message posted to the POD Network electronic mailing list, archived at https://listserv.nd.edu/cgi-bin/wa?A2=ind1006&L=POD&T=0&F=&S=&P=67803

von Wittich, B. (1972). The impact of the pass-fail system upon achievement of college students. *Journal of Higher Education, 43*(6), 499–508. Retrieved April 2, 2010, from http://www.jstor.org/stable/1978896?seq=1

Vosti, K. L., & Jacobs, C. D. (1999). Outcome measurement in postgraduate year one of graduates from a medical school with a pass/fail grading. *Academic Medicine, 74*, 547–549.

Wandersee, J. (2002a). Using concept circle diagramming as a knowledge mapping tool. In K. Fisher, J. Wandersee, & D. Moody (Eds.), *Mapping biology knowledge* (pp. 109–126). Dordrecht, The Netherlands: Springer Netherlands.

Wandersee, J. (2002b). Using concept mapping as a knowledge mapping tool. In K. Fisher, J. Wandersee, & D. Moody (Eds.), *Mapping biology knowledge* (pp. 127–142). Dordrecht, The Netherlands: Springer Netherlands.

Weimer, M. (2002). *Learner-centered teaching: Five key changes to practice.* San Francisco: Jossey-Bass.

Williamson, O. M. (2012). *First-year student time management calculator.* Retrieved October 22, 2012, from http://utminers.utep.edu/omwilliamson/calculator1.htm

Wilson, M. (2008, November). *"Well, little Johnny . . . ."* Session presented at the National Association of Geoscience Teachers (NAGT) Workshops: The Role of Metacognition in Teaching Geoscience, Carleton College, Northfield, MN. Retrieved January 18, 2012, from http://serc.carleton.edu/NAGTWorkshops/metacognition/wilson.html

Wilson, M., Wenk, L., & Mogk, D. (2008, November). *Reflective writing to construct meaning.* Session presented at the National Association of Geoscience Teachers (NAGT) Workshops: The Role of Metacognition in Teaching Geoscience, Carleton College, Northfield, MN. Retrieved January 16, 2012, from http://serc.carleton.edu/NAGTWorkshops/metacognition/tactics/28928.html

Wirth, K. R. (2008a, November). *A metacurriculum on metacognition: Cultivating the development of lifelong learners.* Opening keynote address presented at the National Association of Geoscience Teachers (NAGT) Workshops: The Role of Metacognition in Teaching Geoscience, Carleton College, Northfield, MN. Retrieved January 16, 2012, from http://serc.carleton.edu/NAGTWorkshops/metacognition/wirth.html

Wirth, K. R. (2008b, November). *Learning about thinking and thinking about learning: Metacognitive knowledge and skills for intentional learners.* Session presented at the National Association of Geoscience Teachers (NAGT) Workshops: The Role of Metacognition in Teaching Geoscience, Carleton College, Northfield, MN. Retrieved March 11, 2010, from http://serc.carleton.edu/NAGTWorkshops/metacognition/workshop08/participants/wirth.html

Wirth, K. R. (n.d.). Reading reflections—The role of metacognition in teaching geoscience: Topical resources. Retrieved September 10, 2012, from http://serc.carleton.edu/NAGTWorkshops/metacognition/activities/27560.html

Wirth, K. R., Lea, P., O'Connell, S., Han, J., Gosselin, D., & Ottenhoff, J. (2008, November). *Finding meaning in the introductory science course.* Session presented at the National Association of Geoscience Teachers (NAGT) Workshops: The Role of Metacognition in Teaching Geoscience, Carleton College, Northfield, MN. Retrieved January 15, 2012, from http://serc.carleton.edu/NAGTWork shops/metacognition/group_tactics/28894.html

Wirth, K. R., & Perkins, D. (2005, April). *Knowledge surveys: The ultimate course design and assessment tool for faculty and students.* Paper presented at Proceedings of the Innovations in the Scholarship of Teaching and Learning Conference, Northfield, MN. Retrieved February 7, 2012, from http://www.macalester.edu/ geology/wirth/WirthPerkinsKS.pdf

Wirth, K. R., & Perkins, D. (2008a, November). *Knowledge surveys.* Session presented at the National Association of Geoscience Teachers (NAGT) Workshops: The Role of Metacognition in Teaching Geoscience, Carleton College, Northfield, MN. Retrieved March 11, 2010, from http://serc.carleton.edu/NAGTWork shops/assess/knowledgesurvey/

Wirth, K. R., & Perkins, D. (2008b). *Learning to learn.* Retrieved May 12, 2010, from http://www.macalester.edu/geology/wirth/learning.pdf

Young, J. R. (2011, August 7). Professors cede grading power to outsiders—even computers. *Chronicle of Higher Education.* Retrieved August 8, 2011, from http:// chronicle.com/article/To-Justify-Every-A-Some/128528/

Yu, S., Wenk, L., & Ludwig, M. (2008, November). *Knowledge surveys.* Session presented at the National Association of Geoscience Teachers (NAGT) Workshops: The Role of Metacognition in Teaching Geoscience, Carleton College, Northfield, MN. Retrieved January 16, 2012, from http://serc.carleton.edu/ NAGTWorkshops/metacognition/tactics/28927.html

Zander, R. S., & Zander, B. (2000). *The art of possibility: Transforming professional and personal life.* Cambridge, MA: Harvard University Business Press.

Zimmerman, B. J. (1998). Developing self-fulfilling cycles of academic regulation: An analysis of exemplary instructional models. In D. H. Schunk & B. J. Zimmerman (Eds.), *Self-regulated learning: From teaching to self-reflective practice* (pp. 1–19). New York: Guilford.

Zimmerman, B. J. (2001). Theories of self-regulated learning and academic achievement: An overview and analysis. In B. J. Zimmerman & D. H. Schunk, (Eds.), *Self-regulated learning and academic achievement: Theoretical perspectives* (pp. 1–38). Mahwah, NJ: Lawrence Erlbaum Associates.

Zimmerman, B. J. (2002). Becoming a self-regulated learner: An overview. *Theory Into Practice, 41*(2), 64–70.

Zimmerman, B. J., Moylan, A., Hudesman, J., White, N., & Flugman, B. (2011). Enhancing self-reflection and mathematics achievement of at-risk students at an urban technical college. *Psychological Test and Assessment Modeling, 53*(1), 141–160. Retrieved October 29, 2012, from http://p16277.typo3server.info/ fileadmin/download/ptam/1-2011_20110328/07_Zimmermann.pdf

Zimmerman, B. J., & Schunk, D. H. (2001). *Self-regulated learning and academic achievement: Theoretical perspectives.* Mahwah, NJ: Lawrence Erlbaum Associates.

Zimmerman, B. J., & Schunk, D. H. (2003). Albert Bandura: The scholar and his contributions to educational psychology. In B. J. Zimmerman & D. H. Schunk (Eds.), *Educational psychology: A century of contributions* (pp. 431–457). Mahwah, NJ: Lawrence Erlbaum Associates.

Zubizarreta, J. (2004). *The learning portfolio: Reflective practice for improving student learning*. Bolton, MA: Anker.

Zubizarreta, J. (2009). *The learning portfolio: Reflective practice for improving student learning* (2nd ed.). San Francisco: Jossey-Bass.

Zull, J. E. (2011). *From brain to mind: Using neuroscience to guide change in education*. Sterling, VA: Stylus.

ABOUT THE AUTHOR

Linda B. Nilson is founding director of the Office of Teaching Effectiveness and Innovation (OTEI) at Clemson University and author of *Teaching at Its Best: A Research-Based Resource for College Instructors*, now in its third edition (Jossey-Bass, 2010), and *The Graphic Syllabus and the Outcomes Map: Communicating Your Course* (Jossey-Bass, 2007). She also coedited *Enhancing Learning With Laptops in the Classroom* (Jossey-Bass, 2005) and volumes 25 through 28 of *To Improve the Academy: Resources for Faculty, Instructional, and Organizational Development* (Anker, 2007, 2008; Jossey-Bass, 2009, 2010), the major publication of the Professional and Organizational Development (POD) Network in Higher Education.

In addition, Dr. Nilson has published many articles and book chapters and has presented conference sessions and faculty workshops at colleges and universities nationally and internationally on dozens of topics related to course design, teaching effectiveness, assessment, scholarly productivity, and academic career matters. Her most recent articles document the instability of faculty development careers and serious validity problems with student ratings.

Before coming to Clemson University, Dr. Nilson directed teaching centers at Vanderbilt University and the University of California, Riverside, where she developed the "disciplinary cluster" approach to training teaching assistants out of a centralized unit. She has also taught graduate seminars on college teaching. She entered the area of educational/faculty development while she was on the sociology faculty at UCLA. After distinguishing herself as an excellent instructor, her department selected her to establish and supervise its Teaching Assistant Training Program. In sociology her research focused on occupations and work, social stratification, political sociology, and disaster behavior.

Dr. Nilson has held leadership positions in the POD Network, Toastmasters International, Mensa, and the Southern Regional Faculty and Instructional Development Consortium. She was a National Science Foundation Fellow at the University of Wisconsin, Madison, where she received her PhD and MS degrees in sociology. She completed her undergraduate work in three years at the University of California, Berkeley, where she was elected to Phi Beta Kappa.

143

Also available from Stylus

The New Science of Learning
How to Learn in Harmony With Your Brain
Terry Doyle and Todd Zakrajsek
Foreword by Jeannie H. Loeb

"This is a path-breaking book. Faculty have been learning about how the mind works, and this book spreads the message to students, who need it just as much. More sophisticated and empirically grounded than any study skills manual, this book addresses all the major research findings on how the human brain learns. And it does so using language and examples that students—in fact, anyone with a mind—can easily understand and immediately apply to enhance their attention, depth of processing, retention, retrieval, and far-transfer abilities. The range of learning-relevant topics is impressive: sleep, breaks, chronotypes, exercise, nutrition and hydration, prior knowledge, multisensory (even olfactory) learning, multitasking, pattern identification, mindsets, the malleability of the brain, and more. In addition, the book is *persuasive*. With students' thinking in mind, it documents the costs of sleep and exercise deprivation and makes the fixed mindset look downright unattractive. Plus, each chapter ends with excellent summaries and scholarly references. *The New Science of Learning* deserves to be required reading for all college students—really, anyone interested in learning."

—Linda B. Nilson,
PhD, Director, Office of Teaching Effectiveness and Innovation, Clemson University

Recent advances in brain science show that most students' learning strategies are highly inefficient, ineffective, or just plain wrong. While all learning requires effort, better learning does not require more effort, but rather effectively aligning how the brain naturally learns with the demands of your studies. This book shows students what is involved in learning new material, how the human brain processes new information, and what it takes for that information to stick with them even after the test.

This is not another book about study skills and time management strategies, but instead an easy-to-read description of the research about how the human brain learns in a way that students can put into practice right away.

22883 Quicksilver Drive
Sterling, VA 20166-2102

Subscribe to our e-mail alerts: www.Styluspub.com